Books by Frank Lebell:

HINDSIGHT

THE MANUFACTURERS' REPRESENTATIVE

PROFESSIONAL SALES REPRESENTATION

INDEPENDENT MARKETING/SELLING

SALES AGREEMENT

THIS AGREEMENT made this ___twentieth___ day of ___Februar___ _____ , 19 77

by and between ___Principle Manufacturing Co., Inc___

a corporation incorporated under the laws of the State of ___New York___

having its principal office at ___12578-A Broadway Ave.___

hereinafter referred to as "Manufacturer" and ___Representati___

a corporation incorporated under the laws of the State of ___Cal___

having its principal office at ___1487-B Market A___   ___San Mateo, Calif.___

hereinafter referred to as "Representative", as follows:

MERGER!

1. **Appointment and Acceptance** — Manufactur~ ~its exclusive selling representative to sell products (enumerated in Provision # 3 hereof) in th~ ~on # 2 hereof); and Representative accepts the appointment and agrees to sell and promote th~ ~.oducts.

2. **Territory.** — Representative's Territ~ ~.ing:

3. **Products** — The "products ~ ~.r to be sold by the Representative are:

4. **Amount of Compensation** — Representative's compensation for services performed hereunder shall be _____ % of the "net invoice price" of the Manufacturer's product shipped into Representative's territory. However, when engineering, execution of the order, or shipment involve different territories, the Manufacturer will split the full commission among the Representatives whose territories are involved. The Manufacturer will make this determination and advise the interested Representatives at the time the order is submitted to the Manufacturer. The sum of the split commission shares shall add up to a full commission and no Representative whose territory is involved will receive less than _____ % of the full commission.

5. **Computation and Payment of Commission**

    a) Commissions are due and payable on or before the _____ day of the month following the month in which customer is invoiced; and if not paid when due, the amount not paid will accrue interest at _____ % per annum from the date due until paid.

    b) Manufacturer will send Representative copies of all invoices at the time Manufacturer invoices customer, and each invoice shall indicate the amount of commission due Representative.

    c) At the time of payment of commissions to Representative, Manufacturer will send Representative a commission statement showing:

        i)   the computation of all commissions earned during the ninety (90) day period prior to its issuance (listing all invoice covered by the statement), and

        ii) commissions paid during that period (listing the invoices on which commissions are being paid), and

        iii) commissions due and owing Representative.

"... there is no sharp distinction between where the sales manager leaves off and the sales representative begins. Much of the success they look for in their affiliation is dependent upon the sales manager's realization that the independent sales agent is not an employee but - rather - that he is a specialist in selling, a businessman, and that they have set up a partnership."

- F.L.

Fine point techniques of successful

INDEPENDENT
MARKETING/SELLING

by
Frank Lebell

HILLS-BAY PRESS
P. O. Box 5221
San Mateo, California 94402

Published by
HILLS-BAY PRESS
P.O. Box 5221
San Mateo, California 94402

Manufactured in the United States of America

To Maryan,

with love

CONTENTS

ACKNOWLEDGMENTS

Two organizations stand out among trade associations, specifically devoted to the interests of independent manufacturer's sales representatives and to the sales managements who use the services of these specialists in marketing/selling. They are:

Manufacturers' Agents National Association
2021 Business Center Drive, Irvine, Calif. 92713
"MANA" is long established, a responsible, highly respected organization encompassing members from all industries in which manufacturers' sales agents engage.

*　　　　*　　　　*

Electronic Representatives Association
233 East Erie St., Chicago, Illinois 60611
"ERA" is unilateral, its membership made up of electronic sales representatives, usually technically oriented. The wide ramifications of electronics, its products being employed in so many phases of industry, also has its sales representatives entering fields not necessarily thought of as electronic.

American Arbitration Association
140 West 51st St., New York, N.Y. 10029
"AAA" is a notable, fifty-year-old organization offering arbitration as an alternative to the court system, whereby two parties in dispute submit their claims to a third neutral party for a decision which becomes legally binding.

*　　　　*　　　　*

This writer wishes to acknowledge, with profound thanks, permission of MANA to reproduce the Chart of Accounts article as published in "Agency Sales," its monthly magazine; to ERA for permission to reproduce the salesman's "Expense Report"; to AAA for supplying the information required to describe its procedures and to Mr. Mel Daskal, C.P.A., a partner in the Beverly Hills, California, public accounting firm of Sherman & Daskal who, in the course of many years specializing in serving manufacturers' agents, prepared the referenced Chart of Accounts and Expense Report.

In particular, I want to express my deep thanks to James L. Gibbons, President of MANA, and Raymond J. Hall, Executive Vice President of ERA, for their gracious forewords to this book.   — Frank Lebell

Foreword

The author of "Independent Marketing/Selling" is deservedly termed a professional—and one whose experience as a manufacturers' agent began back in the days when an agency was launched on an uncharted sea with only good common sense as a compass.

The science of marketing through manufacturers' agents and the science of agency operations have come a long way since those days, as this latest work by Frank Lebell so admirably demonstrates—but the need for good common sense and integrity still prevails. The words of guidance, the philosophies as well as the techniques offered in this book are indeed from the heart and experience of a real pro . . .

James L. Gibbons,
President,
Manufacturers' Agents National Association

My sincere thanks, Jim, for your gracious words. And may I congratulate MANA on the high stature it has attained in the business world and its fine leadership, as exemplified in your good self.
— F.L.

Foreword

In the first volume of Frank Lebell's trilogy on manufacturers' sales representation, "The Manufacturers' Representative" he presents the theme, "If you do more things right than wrong, you're a success." That epigram could very well be applied to a trade association's progress. In the case of our Electronic Representatives Association, we started as a small group of friendly competitors back in 1935. Today, we are a large group of friendly competitors — still cooperative, totaling close to 1,500 member firms, with 2,400 offices, employing 9,000 people, responsible for selling six-and-a-half billion dollars worth of electronic products per year. We must be doing *something* right.

Our growth and effectiveness stems from the contributions of time and effort of such volunteers as Frank Lebell. Starting as a rep in 1954, as a one-man organization, putting in night and day to get his business established, he nevertheless found time to be active in working for ERA. He authored the name "Electronic Representatives Association" in 1958, it having been known previously by the cumbersome mouthful, "The Representatives of Electronic Products Manufacturers, Inc."

In the Northern California Chapter of ERA, he served on many committees and officerships, including an unprecedented three terms as president. Nationally, he functioned in numerous capacities, including Chairman of ERA's By-Laws Committee, member of the Government Affairs Committee, etc. Now retired, (ha!) he continues as the Executive Director of our Northern California Chapter and has published (through 1976) the chapter's annual "Directory of Membership and Trade Guide," a publication of over 100 pages, which became a "standard" in our industry.

In "INDEPENDENT MARKETING/SELLING," he dwells on the need for closer cooperation between the sales manager and the sales representative in their common interests, stressing the responsibility of each to the other. He points up that the independent manufacturer's representative, as a sales specialist and small businessman, is capable of fulfilling a big role in successful marketing—proven by the fact that 60-70% of industry's commercial and industrial product is brought to market through manufacturers' representatives.

Frank Lebell's unusual depth of business experience as a one-time distributor, a manufacturer and various other enterprises, largely explains why, in fifteen years, he built a successful sales agency from day "one" to retirement. He writes as one who has been there, indeed as a voice of experience, but as "one of us."

In addition to the new or experienced representative, the sales manager can learn much from studying this author's works. They comprise a comprehensive library of factual, "firing line" experience, an education in the subject of manufacturers' sales representation, written in lucid, easy reading style, often whimsically entertaining. It is indeed a pleasure to recommend Frank Lebell's books.

Raymond J. Hall,
Executive Vice-President,
Electronic Representatives Association

My most sincere thanks, Ray. The enthusiasm and drive you devote to ERA's progress is the kind of spirit that has done so much in making it one of the country's most outstanding trade associations.

—*F.L.*

INTRODUCTION

In its appeal to the more sophisticated — that is, those already established in selling and sales management — INDEPENDENT MARKETING/SELLING is the third volume of a wide-ranging library covering the subject of manufacturers' sales representation. It continues to exemplify the philosophy of that subject as a specialized occupation. In the main, however, the nitty-gritty of this "how-to" is devoted to the honing of fine point skills in independent professional sales people. Techniques presented may be compared to the aiming of a gun: how small the movement required to set it precisely on target and how little it takes to miss! In covering many marketing/selling functions, it rounds out an education for that segment of America's ten and a half million self-employed described as the independent "manufacturers' sales representative" or "sales agent" and popularly known as "the rep." But it is also markedly for the edification of the "sales manager," since the one doesn't function without the other any more than applause is produced by one hand.

For those who think in terms of the functional differences in "moving goods from producer to consumer," "Marketing" may be regarded as a black tie word used to describe locating the prospect, "Selling" as the act of turning him into a customer. Completion of the metamorphosis is best achieved when there exists full, cooperative understanding between the marketing/sales manager and the manufacturers' representative. With that truism in mind, the first few chapters of this work are addressed largely to sales management. The pro/con realities of using the independent professional salesman are fully compared to employing direct, salaried salesmen. Special emphasis points up the practices that make the commission sales agent go and what turns him off.

In completing a trilogy of "how-to" books, of practicality in pursuing the profession of the self-employed sales specialist, INDEPENDENT MARKETING/SELLING is likewise a pragmatic work for the sales executive to study who may be already using or contemplating adoption of the independent, professional salesman system as a viable method of product distribution. With its outspoken commentaries, its insight into the workings of the rep mind, the presumptive thesis of why a book for independent salesmen should also be read by the sales executive is simple:
Shouldn't the man charged with superintending a crew of workmen be fully versed in all aspects of THEIR operation as well as his own?

Much of this volume stems from the author's consultations with sales agents who had growth problems, the need of long entrenched reps for new ideas, sales managers seeking means for establishing more productive rapport with sales people. In the latter case, a f'r instance is the observation that one rarely encounters a sales executive who realizes the main reason a man goes in for independent repping is not *primarily* for the money. It is emphasized that too many marketing executives have barely superficial acquaintance with the commission agent's motivation, that many reps are capable of making more money as company employees than when themselves "self-employed."

As in the counterpoint of music, where distinctly individual melodies are combined to produce enjoyable sound, so it is with interfacing of sales manager and salesman; the harmonious interaction of their respective functions brings out the titillating consonance of bigger and better sales. By the same token, it is pointed out that if the right hand knoweth not what the left hand doeth, the resulting cacaphony is a togethermess. The interlacing of their efforts and the *responsibility* of the one to the other, must be accepted if they are to produce desirable results.

Little more than a grouping of chapters is made to indicate separation between those early chapters addressed specifically to sales executives and the main text intended for sales representatives. This author believes that, in a pragmatic sense, *there is no sharp distinction between where the sales manager leaves off and the sales representative begins.* Their respective activities should dovetail. Much of the success they look for in their affiliation is dependent upon the sales manager's realization that the independent sales agent is not an employee but, rather, that he is a specialist in selling, a businessman, and that they have set up a partnership.

The book is not concerned with rhetoric; it is written in conversational language. With anecdotes or stories sometimes of a wryly humorous nature to illustrate a point, it makes every attempt to avoid the pedestrian, the ponderous and, above all, tries to shun the dreary clichés which seem so often to characterize even the best of "how-to" books. In driving a point home, the author resorts occasionally to composite rather than singled out characters, particularly as in the story addenda, "Only In America." Narration of the protagonist's career demonstrates how life is the institution from which students acquire *summa cum laude* credentials—translated, EXPERIENCE—the background schooling in preparation for entering the profession of manufacturers' representation.

In any event, the bottom line is that the reciprocal action of getting the line (by the rep) and appointing the representative (by the sales manager) mark only the beginning of a joint endeavor whose success is dependent on mutual understanding and respect as they go about carrying on the business óf the "partnership" they have formed. □

BY WAY OF DEFINITIONS

The descriptive terms "manufacturers' sales representative" and "manufacturers' sales agent" (with or without the intervening word "sales") are to be understood as entirely synonymical, despite the author's preference for the first if, as, and when formality is called for. I bow to the widespread interchanging of these terms for identifying the independent professional salesman inasmuch as proponents of either term may have equal justification for preferring the one or the other.

Insofar as my personal predilection for "representative" is concerned, I suppose that is derived from the fact that in the electronic industry, where I had the greater part of my marketing experience, the use of "agent" to describe an independent salesman was passed over from the very beginning of that industry. Perhaps that was because of the word's legal inferences (as independent contractors, we are not authorized to bind the principals). Then, too, "representative" seemed to carry with it a kind of "man of distinction" appeal to this innovative industry. Traditionally, too, except to the uninitiated, the public tends to think of an "agent" as someone in real estate, in insurance or in the spy business.

Further ambiguity now lies in the fact that both "representative" and "agent" are used commonly to include direct employees who may be working in a variety of positions other than sales. To say we are "independent manufacturers' professional marketing/sales representatives" or "sales agents" is telling them like it is, but how often does time permit giving out with a mouthful like that?

It will be noted that the title of this book seems to tacitly accept a difference between "marketing" and "selling." This is in deference to those who set up "Marketing" as a department in itself, distinctly separate from the "Sales Department." Presumably they have reasons. "Webster's Collegiate Dictionary" defines marketing as "an aggregate of functions involved in moving goods from producer to consumer." If you supplement that with describing "the market" as where one's products are sold, it might be presumed *that* makes one who "markets" practically the same as saying one who "sells." Confusing, isn't it?

According to informal estimates, there are thirty-some-odd-thousand independent sales firms (varying from one man to 50 or more individuals per firm). It would seem that someone ought to come up with less awkward terminology descriptive of our profession—hopefully a sharply definitive word or two, preferably eschewing the traditional since ours is a comparatively modern profession made up, in the main, of people characteristically forward looking. A word one is beginning to see something of is "marketer." According to the dictionary, that's what we who "market/ sell" are. (I'd love to see it as "marketeer." Has a kind of romantic connotation, no?)

All of which is by way of leading up to the explanation that, being the author of this book carries with it certain perquisites, such as the privilege of choosing my own verbiology. It will be noted that, in the same spirit as men dispensing with the breath-restraining necktie and ridding ourselves of the blood-constricting leg garter, this writer's wish for comfort extends to using the popular abbreviation "rep" rather than more formal lengthy designations. Certainly one can and should always maintain the image of the respected businessman but keeping in mind that ours is a profession drawing outgoing, friendly people, typically dealing on a first-name basis, ever intent on establishing intimacy with our principals and customers, without necessarily losing dignity. At any rate, begging the reader's indulgence, so far as this writer is concerned, the habits of an adult lifetime are not easily broken.

Ergo—I write as "the rep."

—Frank Lebell

PART I

With philosophical overtones
— as well as bolts-and-nuts . . .

1

WHY DOES A MAN LEAVE
HOME FOR THE UNKNOWN?

Seeking security in the self-employed philosophy

An earnest, thoughtful sales manager might honestly try to understand just exactly why a man would want to pass up the self-evident comforts and comparative tranquility of a presumably good position for the open end uncertainties of the independent manufacturers' sales representative's existence. That executive has much to ponder. To fully understand the attitude, the motivation and the methodology of the professional salesman, will go far toward helping him carry out his own job smoothly and effectively.

The sales manager reflects: the independent rep doesn't have a paternal "home office" to take care of him on the job's working needs. He has no one to supply him with transportation, with gas for the car he had to acquire at his own expense, with secretarial and other office help, with pension contributions for his old age, with unemployment insurance if the country falls into the depths of recession and his business comes to a standstill, or any of the now common, built-in fringe benefits which the employee salesman now counts on as a matter of course.

The sales manager shakes his head, wonderingly: this independent sales agent, a man who has chosen to be in business for himself, electing to sell lines that are compatible but for a number of different manufacturers rather than restrict himself to one employer: no one provides him with anything other than an opportunity to sweat life out on his own.

If he gets an order, he is paid—whoopee!—otherwise, nothing, zilch! He has to maintain his own office, plunk down the rent on the dot, pay the phone bill—all the costs of doing business are on his back. No dependable source of income. Commission checks vary in amount and time of arrival. If business is generally slow, he is the one who has to worry—there's no one to whom he can pass the buck. As compared to the salaried, directly employed salesman, for his place in the sun the rep's life is hop, skip, jump and run from morning to night. **Why be an independent rep?**

Well, the paramount reason is just that: the man wants independence. He responds to the demands of ego, to the creative urge. There are those who just don't have the kind of temperament which enables them to remain cogs in the corporate machine, to perform endlessly mindless, repetitive tasks. They are apt to question orders, especially when issued by a straw boss whose abilities they doubt. They believe wholeheartedly in cooperation, rarely if ever in submission.

Equally compelling—perhaps due to even stronger motivation—for a man to venture forth from the snug harbor of a well-paying job in order to sail vast uncharted seas as his own skipper, would seem paradoxical in that he makes such a choice because he seeks SECURITY from the ebb and flow of business tides. Strange? Knowing he will have to contend with unpredictable conditions and situations awaiting the self-employed? Yet, the reasons he believes his future is best assured by a career as an independent sales agent are not at all complex:

As an employee, a man is vulnerable, his existence at the mercy of wills and determinations over which he has little or no control, subject to a chain of command above him. He is liable to be fired—laid off, is the more polite expression— with minimum or no notice, without regard for what dismissal means to his personal welfare. He has little ground for protest. On the other hand, from the manufacturer's standpoint, the action may seem entirely justified because of some self-preserving need for retrenching, for carrying out a reorganization perhaps to meet recession conditions.

The company's progress may include retaining the man's services but calls for transferring the salesman to a distant territory, leading to uprooting him and his family from familiar and liked surroundings, necessitating the sale of the pleasant home on which so much effort was expanded, to taking the kids out of school, to leaving good friends behind . . .

If he is "let out" and has to hunt for a new position, assuming he really is a good salesman, presumably sooner or later he will find some kind of a new job even, if needs be, at lesser pay than he was earning previously. That is, he may make out all right if he is in his twenties, perhaps if still in his thirties. But if he has ripened into the forties, he encounters the disheartening experiences of dubious questioning about his age. As for his fifties and still needing a job, the ripening has turned him into human garbage—he can forget it—he's dead.

THE SELF-EMPLOYED PHILOSOPHY

1. One enjoys a state of independence. No "boss" to order one about — a man is strictly on his own.

2. He is enabled to put into force his own ideas and methods, without having to "go through channels" in order to try and persuade an employer of his ideas' worthiness.

3. In building his own business, he is responding to man's natural instincts: for creating, for reproducing. Like siring a child, he has conceived and "raises" an enterprise, satisfying his ego.

4. He believes his economic progress will be faster than as a salaried employee, once he has struggled through the first few years as an independent rep. He is willing to make the sacrifices needed in order to be a small but independent businessman.

5. He is in a position to accept or reject the selling of products according to his own evaluations. He is not forced to promote the sale of products in which he does not believe. He knows what he is qualified to do and therefore can apply his talents and abilities accordingly.

6. If he "hits" on a particularly salable product or line, his remuneration becomes correspondingly big practically at once, rather than having to wait on traversing the longer and uncertain route of promotion via "the channels."

7. He can work long or short hours, with full awareness that progress is dependent on himself. If he does well, he can take full credit — if not, he has no one else to blame.

IN SUMMARY: The man who chooses a career in independent manufacturers' sales representation is one who wants to control his own fate and take the consequences. He does, indeed work for the manufacturer but, as one of a distinctive, elite group of specialists. As such, the marketing services of these professionals are made available practically overnight to the smallest as well as to major manufacturers of this country and abroad.   □

2

DIRECTLY EMPLOYED
VS.
INDEPENDENT SALES REPRESENTATIVES

An introduction to Chapter 3

Of course, it must be granted that the directly employed sales force does have its desirable features. It doesn't necessarily follow but it may appear that under some circumstances, certain individualized conditions, perhaps of an engineering nature as in the heavy equipment industry or in the case of some high technology products such as computers, it may appear preferable to take the direct employee route rather than utilize the professional independent salesmen system. Or, it may be just a matter of opinion — or, "Well, that's the way we've always done it."

But otherwise, what of the sales manager beset by the issues involved in maintaining *stability* in his sales force, the sum and substance underlying all other conditions? Perhaps he is fed up with the tremendous costs to his company in time and energy, of searching for and making selections, of finalizing on the new salesman, of training and equipping him, of nursing him to the point of bringing in enough business to be worth his salt — only to have the man leave for a presumably better job and it all has to be gone through all over again. And that is to say nothing of the harassing salesman, importuning for increased pay not particularly warranted, for promotion undeserved, creating commotion with his threatening to quit. High turnover, the need for frequently introducing new faces to the trade, doesn't do the manufacturer any good. What can be done about it? Does the situation call for radical changes in the salesman system?

Trouble is, in deciding on the outside selling principle to be followed, all too often sincere partisans of one selling methodology or the other will fix dogmatically on only one supposedly favorable characteristic, their polemics attributing the greatest importance to this isolated virtue. They stubbornly disregard or overlook features of the other method. In the case of direct versus independent salesmen, it would seem only good judgment and rewarding to make an earnest, thoroughgoing study of the two systems point by point, before coming to a final decision.

In that sense, following is a reprint of a related article on the subject by the author in a recent edition of the annual "MANA" Directory,* which sets out pros and cons of *both* selling methods. Toward the study's end, the writer's conclusions become plain enough but before that the respective two systems for outside sales people are compared — so that the reader can decide for himself.

Published by
* Manufacturers' Agents National Association
2021 Business Center Drive
Irvine, California 92713

3

THE MARKETING/SALES
MANAGER'S DILEMMA

Which way do you go?

The manufacturer's "Director of Sales" or "—of Marketing," for our purpose here embodied in the term, "marketing/sales manager," has scarcely to make a more important, crucial decision that of determining which is the most advantageous PRINCIPLE to follow in choosing outside sales people. *That is: should he cling to the traditional, the long familiar* employee salesman *figure, the man owing all of his working time and allegiance to "the company"—or would that company's interests be better served by the modern day* manufacturers' sales representative, *operating independently as a marketing and sales specialist?*

Many factors enter into the respective philosophies involved—some obvious, others likely to lie below the surface, with pros and cons calling for full exploration by the sales executive.

Is there a preferable way to go? Yes! There is!

1. *The traditional salesman* who, whatever may be the method of remuneration (straight salary plus perhaps with a commission factor, drawing account, year-end profit share—or whatever) is hired on the presumption that he devote all his working time and selling effort to the interests of the *one* company. He functions as an *employee*, subject to orders from the company's superiors—the G.I. of the business world.

2. *The independent manufacturers' sales representative is a specializing small businessman,* acting in behalf of a number of

thoughtfully chosen manufacturers, limited to those he can serve properly. The "principals" he represents are companies varying in ownership but whose products are usually sold to selected divisions of trade within a given category or industry. Self-employed, his remuneration is based solely on a negotiated commission percentage, due and payable only if, as, and when he produces business.

3. Probably not as desirable but sometimes feasible is a combination of forms—that is (a) perhaps salaried employees in some territories, independent reps in others or (b) not too bad an arrangement, wherein an independent rep is paid periodically a fixed sum for pioneering a manufacturer's line, plus a specified commission based on volume of sales produced—such arrangements usually being predicated upon pre-determined time periods, after which the arrangement reverts to a commission only basis.

Sometimes a bemused sales manager, wanting to take advantage of the independent rep system, seeks a rep for a territory with the understanding that commission will be paid on all new business but that certain accounts therein will not carry commissions, they to be considered "house accounts." Though not encountered very often, there have been sales managers even known to accompany such a provision with the condition that those "house accounts" were to be serviced by the rep even though receiving no commission on them.* In fact, a proviso probably accompanying this type of line offering might even be that commissions were not to be

---

* A certain well known, unconscionable sales manager notified one of his reps that a prospective big customer in the latter's territory would be considered a "no commission" account, bluntly admitting that the rep's usual commission was to be passed on in the form of extra discount as an inducement to get the prospect's business. The cognizant rep's response was merely a short, dry suggestion that that over-reaching sales manager consult the company's attorneys about something called the "Robison-Patman Act"—which brought a fast stop to that proposed "unfair favoritism" transgression of the law!

paid until after payment has been duly received by the factory on orders the rep turns in. Unless the rep is inexperienced, pretty desperate for lines or enjoys making like a banker and is willing to help finance such a manufacturer, he will consider that kind of proposal just long enough to say No.

DIRECT FACTORY SELLING

The employee salesman is a familiar figure upon the American scene. His work day is given over to his one principal—"the company." Concentrating upon only one brand and series of products, he comes to be looked upon as expertly versed in the line's qualities, its various usages, its prices as compared to competition. He accepts the policies of his company as a matter of course even though he may disagree with them, taking orders which, if he values his job, he does not dispute.

His territory is defined for him, the class of prospects predetermined; his instructions are to stress certain points in his sales presentation, perhaps to downplay others, and so on—all pretty much as programmed for him by the company executives' planning so that a controlled progression of effort from the heads of the company down to the firing line may be achieved. He has only to get out and make his routine calls on the trade, all concerned hopeful that he will make his presence worth what he costs the company. As an employee ("I only work here") he does not feel he has to bear ultimate responsibility for the company's welfare other than insofar as his job may be immediately affected.

If all goes lovely and he does well, he is looked upon as a permanent member of the organization—that is, until upon reaching his enfeebled gold watch presentation point in time, whereupon "the company" has only to replace him with a younger man whose youthful strengths can be counted on to offset lack of experience and thereafter continues on its corporate way.

That is one side of the picture. Sad to say, an envisioned version of the ideal employee salesman is not that black and white. The company's sales executive must contend with the kaleidoscopic vicissitudes of colorful human nature—and grim realities. Countless difficulties beset the marketing/sales manager seeking to establish a good staff of permanent salesmen, of which the paramount problem is, Where does he find capable, experienced, hard-working men, ready to devote full loyalty to the company's interests in the face of today's increasing disdain for the attractions of "just a job" in the business world? If he is lucky enough to acquire the old-fashioned paragons he seeks, how long can he expect to keep them? What would be his carrot to hold the jackrabbit type who jumps from one job to another? How can he hang on to the ambitious one, to keep his star salesman from leaving for more promising fields inasmuch as the hired hand is here today, there tomorrow—"there" very likely being in the employ of a competitor, since outstanding men are always targets of enticing offers from other companies.

In many cases, either as beginner or even though an experienced salesman, the one newly hired must be put through a training program, to be harnessed into the ways, means, product characteristics and policies of the company. The indoctrination process is costly in itself, with expenses merrily running right along while waiting for the new man to start pulling his weight.

As may easily happen, a very wrong man is inadvertently hired. It can—and does happen. Usually, only after a lapse of time, does the damage he inflicted become evident. Perhaps it's a personality grating on customers that didn't show up when he was being interviewed for the job—he turning out to be a bumbling character, who loses trade by frequently making errors in customers' requirements.*

---

* An historic instance of what makes a sales manager's hair turn prematurely gray was that of the newly-hired hand who abruptly lost the

He could be one of those self-enjoyed comics who offers allegedly funny lines in lieu of making sales points, who tells ethnic jokes without regard for their harmful effect, the kind who would also be oblivious to coughing spells induced in a buyer by clouds of smoke emanating from his cigarette or pipe. Or—and certainly common enough—he can be one who goldbricks on the company's time, chisels on his expense account and in a variety of ways, brings to the job some of the more flagrant failings of being a human being.

INDEPENDENT MANUFACTURERS' REPRESENTATION

A sharp contrast to such strains on a sales executive's blood pressure and the company's well-being would be to utilize the independent manufacturers' representation form of marketing/selling. In that case, the manufacturer starts right in with one tremendous advantage—namely, that selling cost is always a fixed percentage directly related to sales; he pays only for business actually placed in his hands. No need to deplete capital so useful in other ways by continuing to hand out checks to salesmen who, on account of recessions, inroads of competition, incompetence or whatever the reasons, are not producing business.

The trials and tribulations of searching for good men, the need to train salesmen, with its time-consuming costs, with all the accompanying expenses and aggravations—all are eliminated. The independent rep firm comes right in to the manufacturer's operations with a ready-to-go staff of trained,

---

business of an old, highly valued customer by a casual quote from the price list in his sales book. It was later learned by the man who eventually replaced him that the buyer, startled, had exclaimed the price quoted was something like a third higher than he was accustomed to paying, that the salesman had stoutly proclaimed there had been a price increase, with a lofty wave pointing out that "everything was going up."

The dolt had not read to the bottom of the price list page, where the 40% trade discount was shown!

outside salespeople, with an office staff for backup, all at no cost to its principals unless and until orders are brought in. The head of the rep firm functions as a regional sales manager, his services included in the bargain without further cost. The burdens of employee prerogatives—vacations to be paid for, the insurance, the auto maintenance, the pensions, the social security contributions with their accompanying tedious record keeping and mandatory government reports—all are borne by the independent rep firm.

A most important fact to be considered is that the independent rep stems from an already *cultivated* territory wherein, ipso facto, if he has been existing there, it stands to reason he must be in favor with the customers—obviously, he wouldn't be eating regularly if he weren't producing business for his principals! Nobody provides unemployment insurance for *him*! If the product or line is new, or otherwise is a line requiring building up, he has only to take it to trade where he is already favorably known, an accepted supplier, to key procurement individuals with whom he has probably long been on a first-name basis, and short-cutting directly to the kind of trade which his experience and familiarity with the territory tells him would be of interest in such offerings.

Then there is the so-called department store philosophy, wherein the reps presents a variety of products, enabling the buyer to conveniently consider the products of a number of lines, enabling him to think in terms of obtaining several or perhaps many of his requirements from the one source, with consequent savings in time and perhaps money—the attractions of each line helping draw attention to the others. By the same token, with his entire roster of lines to bear expenses, the rep gets into remote and sometimes quite isolated areas to which the one-line salaried salesman could not afford to travel profitably.

Perhaps most important of all, is the unusual *kind* of man who goes in for independent manufacturers' representation. That is an occupation which takes great courage, self-confidence and a tremendous capacity for working hard. By the very nature of his chosen vocation, the rep must be a self-starter, with self-motivation that requires no prodding to "get out there and get to work!"

As an entrepreneur, the rep is one of the country's "small businessmen." He is himself an executive in every sense of the word, fully cognizant of problems from behind the desk as well as out in the field. He is driven by a need to produce maximum business from *each* of his lines. Because of limited manpower, he *must* work his lines hard if, for no other reason, the fact that *he* has undertaken all those selling expenses of which he has relieved the manufacturer.

For such reasons and more, the manufacturer receives the benefit of the rep's ten, twelve and sometimes longer number of hours per day devoted to his work. Contrast that kind of preoccupation with the all-too-prevalent attitude of the employee type of salesman reflecting the feeling that he owes his job only a fixed number of hours a day, limited to so many days a week, culminating in such-and-such a rate of pay per unit of time! In one sense, the independent, a modern-day specialist, can be looked upon as a throwback, a practitioner of a very old-fashioned, almost extinct philosophy—that know-how and hard work are basic to success.

In considering the independent manufacturers' representation system, it may be that some kinds of products do not lend themselves to this selling principle. One reason could be because of exceeding complexity combined with very high prices, calling for in-depth engineering proficiency to demonstrate their features with prospects few and far between. Such products, entailing large capital expenditures, would probably be subject to long drawn-out studies and discussions in upper echelons of the prospective customer, as well as buyers. The time factor involved, in itself would seem to make it impractical for the self-employed rep to engage in such business profitably.

Yet—even in such circumstances, in some cases it is possible to make arrangements for utilizing the independent rep system advantageously. I am referring to the quite pragmatic use of the rep in a bird-dogging or "finding" capacity. As an example of how beautifully such an arrangement worked out for both parties, from this writer's own experience:

Though "repping" in the electronic industry, we had acquired representation of a line of shock mounts and vibration controls, products seemingly remote from our usual trade category but, as a matter of fact, often required in electronics, to help protect sensitive equipment and to overcome vibration problems in the holding of delicate instrument adjustment.

Knowing our territory, we would dig lustily for situations requiring applications of such controls, very much enamored by visions of large commission potentials in that such installations were usually big ticket items, often running into the thousands, and at 10% commission . . . ! Then, too, we had that wonderful incentive, so gratifying to a rep, of having a very cooperative factory to back us up. That would lead to this typical situation:

The incredibly fine resolution of a costly, high-powered laboratory microscope could be rendered all but useless by vibration. A common recourse would be to mount it on a brick foundation for apparently solid support, or cushion it on a layer of inflated auto inner tubes, the users thus hoping to eliminate disturbing vibration.

That such makeshift arrangements were of little value was due to the fact of the earth itself acting like a kind of great spring, always in minute but constant motion, and of course such movement is transmitted through whatever rests on its surface. The manufacturer we represented had developed a special vibration control unit which dissipated the disturbing forces produced by the trembling earth *before* they reached the microscope so that the instrument would be kept completely inert, thus with no loss of its resolution features.

Our deals worked like this: upon locating such juicy possibilities, we would notify the factory. Since there were hardly ever any two sets of conditions exactly the same and applied technology was always necessary, they would fly out one of their highly qualified engineers to the scene of action. That expert would take the problem in hand, drawing up the applicable specs, making recommendations as to models, possible deviations and so on. After his departure, we then had only to make the usual follow-up calls. In due time, when the order came through, the commission involved was something gladsome to contemplate because, as indicated before, such equipment didn't come for cheap! It was an example of how bird-dogging interfaced with a cooperative manufacturer, served to produce many mutually profitable deals.

SUMMARY

I am sure that by now the author's bias is showing. Well, with due allowance for variations in individual competence, and taking all factors into consideration, in my opinion the sales manager who chooses to stay with a staff of employee sales people rather than to utilize the professional services of the independent rep system, is failing to take advantage of modern day's specialization in commercial endeavor. Since it is considered standard practice now for manufacturers to buy so many of the parts needed for their products from those who specialize in making such items, rather than trying to manufacture all under one roof, why doesn't the principle similarly hold true by utilizing benefit of representatives who are *sales specialists* in their respective territories?

If that sales manager were to employ empathy, study the commissioned rep concept in detail, he would gain an eye-opening revelatory understanding and insight into why a man leaves the comfort, the presumed security and privileges of a good-paying job to plunge into the struggle, the hardships, the tougher occupation of independent manufacturers' representation, and why *that* kind of man would bring him better results than the salaried salesman.

No one is going to deny that the independent rep is a human being who also could be subject to the kinds of faults that may afflict the directly employed salesman. Of course! It takes all kinds! Naturally, good judgment in making selections must be used. But, one cannot over-emphasize the fact that the independent rep *has* to do better than the salaried man in order to exist. An employee type may switch and drift from job to job, his meandering interrupted only by rest stops to pick up checks at the unemployment office, but the self-employed has no such prerogatives. He has, himself, put himself on the spot — he has had to acquire the skills in sales technology that will enable him to do well by his principals and customers, or else . . .

And as such, for those sales managers who will take the time and trouble to study the self-employed marketing/salesman system and learn how best to work with these specialists, it will be found that the independent manufacturers' sales representation system is the better way to go. □

4

ONE-MAN OPERATION
VS.
THE DEPARTMENT STORE SYNDROME

Small firm or multi-man group

A manufacturer employing the independent professional salesman system has need for representation in a given territory with, let's say, an annual potential volume ranging anywhere from five hundred thousand dollars to perhaps several times that. The question arises: should he appoint a one or two-man and girl operation or would a multi-employee agency be preferable?

There are many significant factors to be considered, some not obvious.

At first glance, one would very likely lean toward the firm employing a substantial number of people because of presumed wide coverage of the trade. Such a multi-man sales force (and, of late, certainly including women in many instances) presents what one might describe as "the department store syndrome." A woman shopping in Macy's for bedsheets has her attention drawn to a display of attractive blankets and pillow cases of a colorful design, sees a new style digital alarm clock on a handsome nightstand alongside of the display, and winds up buying several bedroom items.

In short: the "buyer" — which she is, in our language — has been *exposed* to many items which were not included in the initial purpose of entering the store, thus leading to building up the sales dollar volume as a result of only one "call"—so to speak. In our case, the rep salesman, with his binder of numerous catalogs describing his roster of lines, manages in one way or another to draw the prospect's interest to lines or items aside from the original subject of his call. Multiply such sales people out in the field, calculate the impressive total of calls they make, the variety of opportunities arising for introducing products other than involved in the original reason for being there so that, as in the case of the department store displays, it all adds up to our manufacturer purporting to get a preponderance of coverage from a multi-man rep agency which apparently the small one or two-man operation can't equal.

In addition, just the very size of the rep company in itself is presumed to be impressive to the buyer. That "they sell everything" he knows is a loose exaggeration but, nevertheless, the buyer is likely to think of "that big outfit" as a first source for a new requirement. He may feel that such a big company is more reliable than a small outfit and therefore more likely to take responsibility for his interests. As in the case of the mass circulating medium for advertising, or a man of huge muscular proportions engaged in professional sports, the aura of size carries with it an inference of superior capability.

Also, a meaningful benefit of selecting the services of the large rep firm is the assumption that its head would have to be a man of outstanding business abilities to have built up such a big operation, and that his principals therefore would get this executive's services as a regional manager without cost. Then, too, a manufacturer new to the scene may expect to have his line introduced throughout the referenced territory by virtue of the fact that the veritable department store, the multi-manned firm, supposedly covers the area like a blanket. A certain amount of immediate acceptance by the trade rubs off on him due just to the very fact that this large, widely known rep firm has agreed to represent and sell his products alongside of their already well known lines.

But human nature's tendency to automatically attribute marks of excellence or high stature to bigness, per se, runs counter to an oft-demonstrated truth, the one about big values come in small packages—as witness, the diamond.

THE "SMALL" REP OPERATION

In considering the virtues or drawbacks of the small rep firm, it is of primary importance to take into consideration the background of the one or two men forming the enterprise. There is no such thing as "a born salesman" any more than one can be a born violinist. It can be reasonably believed that the man who struck out for himself as an independent rep must have had considerable experience in selling or, if in a high technology field, has at least been drawn to marketing by virtue of having been a highly placed engineer or some form of executive accustomed to reps working with him. He has been, in many cases, a purchasing agent, a one-time distributor or even a sales manager himself. Versed in the vicissitudes of manufacturers' representation, it took courage and aggressiveness to chose a career in that risky, self-dependent occupation. For the manufacturer, to begin with, that means a man of character, of maturity, in turn one to impress the trade with his personality, thereby to make a favorable impression for the principal.

It should be obvious that in the man who has gone into business for himself, the sales manager has an agent personally representing his company to the trade whom he, himself selected—a situation entirely different from trusting to a rep employer's "associates." Unlike the "associate" (i.e., employee) who has his evenings, weekends and holidays to spend on his personal interests, in the case of the man in business for himself, it is his entire livelihood and then some that is at stake. Every line he takes on must produce — or else! He can't just quit if the going is rough or he is disinclined to work hard — he *has* to make good. He can't start another enterprise if he folds up on this one; it's not in the stars.

As for the big firm's much-vaunted wide coverage: it is quite possible that the manufacturer represented by the small firm may get *better* coverage than when the line is placed with the big rep company. If the "big" company has fifteen or twenty salesmen out calling on trade, other than under most unusual circumstances, it is most unlikely that one's line is being sold by all those people.

The respective lines are apportioned among the sales staff according to their aptitudes, their personal qualifications. One kind of product is more likely to be sold by one than by another. Thus, in the main, a given line is assigned to a limited number of the company's sales people — in short, the roster is departmentalized, with probably no more salesmen specifically out plugging a given line than if it had been placed with a small rep firm.

In the case of the one-man firm, of necessity the rep has to limit the *number* of lines to what he himself can handle, particularly requiring that they be compatibles so that one may open the door to sales for another. Whereas (with some certain exceptions) the "big" company has to have a large roster of lines in order to support its proportionately high overhead.* It is manifest then that the small rep must give

---

* Of course there are some product lines so big and remunerative! in themselves that, obviously, it takes a considerable number of sales people just to work that one line. This writer knows of one such case wherein the rep company employs some fifteen "associates" whose entire efforts are devoted to that line. Such a group can scarcely be considered under the heading of the usual manufacturers' representation. A firm like that is practically a captive. For all pragmatic purposes, in effect such a "rep company" must be an integral (certainly not an "independent") department of that manufacturer's operations rather than an entity in itself. (Great deal for the principal — all the advantages of an obedient, salaried sales force — without the salaries and "fringe" benefits!)

each line the closest attention, to be worked strongly, in depth, because livelihood, his ability to get on in the world, to make his waking time per day give utmost value, depends on what he himself produces. He *can't* goldbrick because he'd be fooling no one but himself. □

5

TIT FOR TAT

— The agent and principal appraise each other

When a sales manager and a prospective rep size each other up — perhaps as they approach the sales agreement negotiation stage — there are fine points to be determined by both parties not readily visible to the naked eye. If the appointment of a sales agent results from simply an exchange of letters or a brief interview, such as at a trade show, there isn't much more than luck to determine how the arrangement is going to turn out. Since so many rep appointments are made with only that perfunctory degree of judgment, you have right there one of the reasons why turnover in the handling of some lines is notoriously and unnecessarily high.

FROM THE STANDPOINT
OF THE MANUFACTURER

1. For a lasting affiliation, you just have to devote a reasonable amount of time and effort to the task before finalizing on the appointment of a new sales representative. (The singular, as used here, is intended to include the entire personnel of a rep firm). For one thing: why not canvass *the last word* on whether or not the firm you are considering is the right one — by referring, namely, to the customer? A few judicious enquiries among customer buyers is likely to provide you with some thought-provoking opinions of how your prospective representative might be expected to fare in getting results for you — a kind of Nielsen rating thing.

2. I wouldn't give much for a sales agreement arrived at without a personal, exploratory conference. Either the sales manager should visit the territory under consideration in person, and stay long enough to gather sufficient evidence for making sound judgments or, even better if halfway decided, invite the prospective rep to visit the factory. In the latter event, much of future mutual value would be in sight for him to observe, to absorb, to carry back with him for future use.

Obviously, the matter of travelling cost in the latter case arises. This is a matter of opinion or policy but if the manufacturer doesn't feel he wishes to pay the applicant's expense, he should at least agree to something on the order of a 50-50 split. When it comes right down to it—how much is a good sales representative worth to you? In the long run, the travelling expense of interviewing a representative who will turn out well is nominal when that is all that stands in the way of getting one of the better sales agents—or by the same token, saves you from appointing a dud! It should be most meaningful when you meet the prospective rep face-to-face, to realize that the impression he makes on you is what your customers will get if he represents your line.

3. Which brings up the question of *who* is actually to make the rep firm's calls. Is it this head man, the one whom you meet and get to know something about? Or is it going to be the firm's Tom, Dick or Harriet "associates" who are going to contact *your* prospect trade, who are going to tell the people *they* represent your company? In other words: you should meet the individual sales people who, in actual fact, will make the calls soliciting business on your behalf. They should be looked over (preferably interviewed) extensively enough for you to form judgment of their personalities, their capabilities.

4. An important detail, usually passed over as nominal: who answers this rep firm's phone and how? If someone who is interested in *your* line calls the rep's office with a view to

getting information about your products, what kind of reception will he receive? Warm, pleasant, informative? Or a laconic, disinterested, barely civil response? Not too important? Phone receptionists are out of your bailiwick? Oh? Really? Can't you visualize a desirable would-be customer of *yours* phoning the rep's office with the intention of making some enquiry or other, perhaps to be poorly handled and, disgruntled, be driven to competition for his requirements? Hasn't it happened to you?

Try phoning your prospective rep's office (before the gal has learned to recognize your voice), to ascertain whether or not a caller gets reasonably fast and proper attention and chalk that up as one more pro or con in sizing up your prospective representative. (Incidentally, speaking of women — if it should happen that this rep's rating in Heaven is such that he is blessed with having a good secretary, and one who presumably is going to stay with him, give that firm a great big plus because that gal can be worth more to the business than some of these outside super-duper salesmen. Try to learn if she is being paid according to her worth, by way of being assured she will stay. Women are finally beginning to come into their own — at least in the way of remuneration for what they are really worth — but there are men around who still don't realize the century has turned!)

5. Now, it is quite possible that your unending war with the clock-and-calendar precludes giving this all-important matter of selecting a well qualified sales agent all the time you should. Not only that, but your interests might be better served by paying for the services of those who have the training, the skills and the resources for bringing good possibilities to you. In that event, you might be best off by turning your requirements over to someone like the long-established Albee-Campbell, a Pennsylvania company specializing nationally in selecting sales agents for their manufacturing clients or some similar organization offering a "recruiting" service.

FROM THE AGENT'S POINT OF VIEW

From where the rep stands, the outlook is different. He has little ground for laying down mandatory conditions. On the other hand, his selling skills, familiarity with the trade—in short, his all-round qualifications and the fact that the manufacturer *needs* good representation in the territory, combine to give him a reasonable amount of leverage for achieving his aims.

Just what would be a sales agent's dream line? In its major aspects, that's easy. All he wants is the kind of line that consists of attractive products, of a kind widely used in his marketing category, plentiful supplies of comprehensive well organized and nicely printed literature, the products competitively priced, promoted by plenty of advertising, headed by a cooperative sales manager and — oh yes — carrying a substantial commission rate. (Well, one can dream, can't one?)

But, there's more. There are points with sharp differences possible between manufacturer and rep on which one is liable to be impaled. A common example: by every standard of good business, the rep should receive his commission on a regular, pre-determined basis. As set up by most legitimate manufacturers now — unfortunately not by all — commission checks on orders shipped are mailed as of a specific date of the month following the month of shipment. That should so state flatly in the sales agreement—the only qualification being that in the event a customer fails to pay, the rep is to be charged back for that portion of his commission. It is an absolute must that he have his commissions at dependable dates in order to take care of his cash flow.

Another potentially sore point on which there should be preventative mutual understanding: does the principal expect his reps to man his booth at trade shows? They should not be asked to do so. The rep pays his own way to the show, he has a number of principals perhaps holding sales meetings, should be using his time to study the exhibits (especially those of competitors!), greeting customers on the floor and steering them to his principals' booths and so on. It is not productive for a rep to have to be anchored in a booth, talking with people from all over the country with whom he can't expect to have any further dealings—with visitors who, in any event, are there to meet factory people, not agents whom they can see any old time.

Something that most definitely should be anticipated and agreed upon is the potential split-commission situation. This is a subject on which manufacturers and agents may differ widely and vehemently if it is not foreseen. The exact terms of a split-commission should be set out explicitly in the sales agreement. The rep ought not to allow himself to have the blah-blah experience I once had to accept because this point was not provided for in one of my rep contracts:

> *In my earlier years, I was calling on a then comparatively new but highly publicized, prestigious Research Laboratory (that very modern showpiece which was a highlight of Krushchev's visit here). I introduced the product at this Lab. I secured the necessary involved engineering data for them and submitted samples.*
>
> *I racked up many miles, driving back and forth on follow-ups. The product was given their thoroughgoing engineering tests. Eventually, it was approved. The production order that followed, however, was issued by one of their Eastern plants, a couple of thousand miles from my territory, where it was incorporated in their equipment. One of my good contemporaries, an agent whom I didn't even know by name, had a beautiful windfall, dropped right in his lap. Me? Not so much as a word of thanks—from anybody!*

Of course, it would have to be expected that in dealing with such widespread corporations, the rep who inherits the benefit of another's work in all probability has to do some servicing at his end and rightfully could expect some compensation. Under similar circumstances, that would be true in most any case, especially of lines encompassing high technology products, specialized machinery, heavy power tools, elaborate systems or just about any big ticket test equipment and so on. But the real, the meaningful work is done at the designer engineering level. The representative who secures the complete engineering specifications has done a major part of the selling end of the job.

In other words, one would think that a fair split in commission ought to be largely in favor of the rep who has worked with the prospect's research and engineering groups, whereas the actual writing out and issuing of the order from a head office in some distant city would call for a smaller percentage to be paid to the rep in that territory. In general—as so often happens when dealing with large corporations—the engineering is done in one part of the country and production in another—in all justice adding up to at least a 50-50 split between the two reps involved, rather than it all be handed over to the rep in whose territory the order is issued.

Of course, much depends on the character of the principal involved, and how fair he is willing to be in including equitable provision in the sales contract that would cover this contingency. They're not all like the one back of the situation I just related. Some years later, I was calling on Hewlett-Packard, the Mt. Olympus of the electronic world. I had been selling them large quantities of a certain product —getting regular, lovely orders, months in-months out. There were occasional problems—the account calling for considerable servicing, many conferences with the senior project engineer of that section—necessitating considerable investment of time and activity on my part—but the monthly commission check amply repaid me.

One day, the sun was knocked out of the sky with the announcement that H-P was building a new plant in Colorado, many miles from the head plant in Palo Alto—far from my territory. They would be shifting production of the units in which my product was designed to that distant plant! Oh, woe was me! Well—it was nice while it lasted!

But, lo and behold! Hewlett-Packard doesn't need any plug from me but, as one who called on them for many years, who came to know many of their staff, I think a pretty good indication of how this company does business is that they gave their vendors as much consideration as they did customers. In my case, the following is only one example:

Unbeknownst to me, their purchasing manager wrote a personal letter to the president of the referenced principal. I saw a copy of it afterwards, or I would not have believed it. In effect, he said that whoever the manufacturer's rep would be was not for H-P to say, of course, but that, if they were to lose the assistance and services of Frank Lebell in their Palo Alto plant because of shifting production to their new Colorado plant, in connection with further orders for that B__ M__ (product), "it would probably be necessary to find another source of supply." . . . Result? The principal saw to it that I was satisfactorily compensated for the next two years!

One of the more common situations calling for thoughtful decision is when the established sales agent is contacted by a new manufacturer seeking representation in his territory. The product looks attractive, useful and seems to be priced about right. But the manufacturer is small, unknown, hasn't sufficient capital for an advertising campaign, not even for a decent catalog. In effect, the rep is being asked to subsidize him by virtue of supplying his own time and effort in the marketing of this new product, with little more than some envisioned far-off possibility of being repaid *after* he has built the line up. On the face of it, though perhaps regretfully because the product does look good, he had best pass the line up. At that point, it is not to the rep's interest or his problem.

But suppose the manufacturer has been at it long enough to be considered reasonably well established. In one way or another, he has built up some going business. It is no longer a garage operation; he is now housed in perhaps a small but fairly well equipped plant, with something upwards of several employees. In short — he's in business — for real — no mistake about it.

The first and perhaps the most meaningful portent of that manufacturer being on the way is: does he have good, informative, well printed literature now — including a catalog attractive enough so that prospects are not *distracted* by thinking about how it was printed? In other words, if it's a cheap, poorly printed job, they'll notice *that* and the impression, perhaps subconscious, won't be good. If it's well printed, the trade is so used to receiving good examples of that old art, they won't pay much attention to how the catalog is printed but their thinking is then directed to its contents — which is where you want it.

This time, if you now have the opportunity, you might give that line consideration. The people heading things up are personable, have well warranted beliefs in their future, seem to know what they are doing. They have a number of reports or testimonials from users of their products, indicating high approval, their commendations evidently justified. You make a few prudent enquiries about the line's attractions among a few of your old customers whose judgment you've learned to value and they speak of it with some approval. From all you can gather, it's a promising line, ready for development, growth and expansion. You now believe it would make a productive addition to your roster.

At this point in time, the manufacturer is quite flexible in agreeing to details of a sales agreement because he's so anxious to have sales people out plugging his products.

Once that line is fully established, well known and selling in goodly volume, he may not be so quick to conform to the conditions under which you like to operate. Furthermore, there are those who would begin clamping down as soon as they have had some success—cutting commission rates, perhaps even supplanting the agents who built them up with their own, supposedly lower cost, direct sales people.

While you still have the chance—assuming you want the line—*you* draw up the sales contract. There is no reason at all why this should be unfair to the other party, but make it hard and fast in covering all the essentials, especially such specifications as those which refer to **termination conditions**. Do this at the time you first negotiate your agreement with this principal—otherwise, you have no assurance that the time, money and experience you invest in building this line up will be properly repaid *afterwards*. (If you, Mr. Reader, happen to be a sales manager or equivalent thereof, don't feel irritated by the foregoing hard-nosed advice—it is from bitter experience. If the established rep hasn't already had reason to realize the validity of such precautions, he will. It behooves the rep to consider that it takes all kinds to make a world.)

Some agreement must be reached on the frequency, length and form of market feed-back to the factory. Not to repeat what I have written about elsewhere at length on this sticky point but, just in a word, all concerned should be made aware that the rep's raison d'etre is to be out in the field selling—not sitting at his desk writing about it.

Home office backup, plentiful supplies of informative, well designed and attractively printed literature, authoritative factory people making trips into the field to work with the rep, adequate samples furnished, fast answers fully responsive to the enquiries and questions emanating for the rep—yea, verily, the sales manager who gold plates his line

with such goodness, may rightfully expect to be showered
with heavenly manna in the form of many big fat orders,
and from customers who discount their bills.

So may it be!   ☐

6

THE OVER THIRTY AND OUT

Baloney!

In his "As You Like It," it took Shakespeare all of "seven ages" to describe a man's life—from the "infant mewly and puking" through "the schoolboy, the lover, the soldier" and so on to the final "second childishness, sans everything." But with our modern sense of dispatch, we summarily size a guy up with an approving he's "under thirty" or a devastating "over thirty" and that's it. Just like that.

I have no fight with youth. Nothing is wrong with youth that the years won't cure. There are pictures of me around to prove I was young once myself—and here I am, managing to have outlived it. Nor do I have any personal cause to serve in the business world, since I stand on the sidelines of that war now. What follows, then, in discussing today's cult of youth, is a strictly objective opinion on admittedly a very controversial subject which has much application in considering manufacturers' representation.

In the human scheme of things, there is properly a joyous place and time for the young, but one of mankind's most misleading delusions is the assumption that the magic carpet of youth must necessarily change into an all-enveloping, smothering blanket with the passing of the years. One commonly encounters the attitude that those who have passed thirty have passed on, gone into final mortality insofar as the business world is concerned. It is the philosophy expressed by a scornful dismissing, "When they're over thirty, they've had it."

If that is used with reference to manufacturers' representation—bull-bleep!

I suppose a case of sorts might be made out for being under thirty as a mandatory requirement if one is thinking of prize fighting, running the 100-yard dash in less than ten seconds or digging of trenches—as in wars. Oh, of course, no doubt there are many occupations in which the strength of a man's biceps is more important than his brain power.

But we're talking about manufacturers' sales agents.

We hear much admonition concerning the waste of energy nowadays. In a country notorious for wastefulness, one of our most stupid profligacies is waste of human energy—as witnessed in the bypassing of the over-thirty-year-olds, ascribing to those poor forty- and fifty-year-olds enfeeblements calculated to have them ready for the garbage heap of the business world. The artisan having lived long enough to learn how to use the tools of his trade with skill, is now discarded in favor of the apprentice! The mere fact that the young fellow is full of "p. & v." is far from being a handicap but that doesn't necessarily make him a good rep any more than in the case of a likable man becoming successful as a rep just because he has a pleasant personality. It takes more — oh, so much more!

In 1974 there were 42 million Americans over 55 and it is projected that more than half our population will be over 55 by the year 2000. It is worthy of note, just to cite a few more numbers, that Ben Franklin was 83 when he invented bifocal glasses, Peter Cooper built the first American locomotive and then ran for President of the United States at 85, Tom Edison, who died at 84, had patented more than 1,000 inventions including the light bulb, the automatic telegraph and the phonograph by that time. And, of course there were many others rated genius who did great things as old men.

But alas, in all fairness, it must be acknowledged we don't live that long nowadays either—what with our air and water pollution, too many calories from eating foods lacking in good nutrition, the cholesterol thing, airplane crashes, a lot of wars in recent years and all that. And I am not suggesting that decrepit, doddering old members of the prune juice set make better reps, in face of the self-evident fact that the rigors of repping most certainly require reasonably good physical condition. Manufacturers' representation can be a rough, tough, exhausting occupation. You have to be out in the field, stumping the hustings, running the highways from customer to customer, racing to the airport to meet incoming sales managers, competing vigorously with countless rivals for new business, fighting off the attempts of competitors to steal your customers, putting in ten, twelve, or even more hours per day in order to keep up with it all.

But the fact is that the healthy, robust man in his forties, fifties and, in a good many cases, even in his sixties, in good health, has *high priority advantages* which only the years can bring to manufacturers' representation. In its January 8, 1976 issue, *TIME*, the weekly magazine, reported, "Elderly people are no less creative or mentally alert than anyone else . . . A person over 65 has an average of 1.3 acute illnesses a year, compared with 2.1 a year for all ages."

I have to tell you the true story of an "over thirty" rep, the philosophy in his case being particularly meaningful when it is realized that his main experience after reaching "way over thirty" has been in a fantastic high technology industry—namely, electronics. Visualize the mind-boggling progress of that industry, propelled by a rocket-like series of technical explosions from homemade crystal radio sets with coils wound on oatmeal cartons to an automated, computerized world clocked by "chips" holding ten thousand transistors in two-tenths of an inch instead of springs—all but incredible developments of within no more than the past half century.

It was in this industry, youthful in itself, at the age of fifty-five, with only an elementary knowledge of electronic technology, that our subject opened his first office as an independent manufacturers' representative. Now, by this "over thirty" complex, it would seem ludicrous for a man of that age, in so dynamic an industry, to try and be a rep. Someone said of him, "The guy has to have a lot of guts or rocks in the head!" Well, presumably he had both—but what the speaker should not have overlooked was that, additionally, the object of his derision *had been an experienced businessman.* He had been engaged for some years in manufacturing, had been a wholesale distributor, an employer of many people in several enterprises, an office manager and outside salesman in a couple of old, long-established industries—in short: he had years and years of life's training, *preparation*, a background of deep *experience* for the wide requirements of being a sales agent. He had only to continue what to him was known as merchandising, though many people nowadays give it either the wider-sounding, formal, black-tie name *marketing*; others know it by the plebeian word, *selling*.

Why is experience so especially necessary in manufacturers' representation? Why, as in many other industries, isn't "on the job training" feasible?

The independent manufacturers' sales representative is one of the country's so-called "small businessmen," of the kind that represent the "free enterprise" principle of America. As such, he is charged with knowing that selling consists of more than simply barging into a buyer's office and asking him to buy something. He needs sufficient judgment to evaluate the unfavorable as well as the good features of a line, to carry out the administration of a business, to properly gauge the competence of employees and to train them, to envision the possible office distractions of a prospective secretary possessed of overly attractive lines herself. In effect, he is a regional sales manager, needing to know how to handle hot situations, such as to recognize and act on the signs that an old customer is becoming a dubious credit risk, another is threatening to sue because of being damaged by an overdue delivery, still a third is cancelling his business because of being mishandled by the factory, etc., etc.

"THE MANUFACTURERS' REPRESENTATIVE IS MORE THAN A COMMISSIONED SALESMAN. HE'S A TERRITORY MANAGER ... A PERSONNEL MAN-AGER ... A CUSTOMER SERVICE MANAGER ... A SALES MANAGER ... A PRODUCT MANAGER ... A MERCHANDISING MANAGER. *AND AN INDEPEN-DENT BUSINESSMAN!*   — *Electronic Representatives Association*

Nobody is born with those abilities! They are acquired only with maturity!   □

7

THE TEN-FOOT PIP-SQUEAKER

— Why a rep may be forced to resign a good line

In this somewhat less than perfect world, a rep trying to achieve a state of well-being, sometimes has his struggles compounded by an occasional sales manager of the kind whose mental myopia causes him to see himself looming up as ten feet tall. Fortunately, such executives aren't common — but they do exist. One certain rep, grown weary of continued confrontations with one of that pip-squeak mentality, gave way to being human and decided to end it all by writing a letter of resignation.

His wording was politely formal, with vague allusions to cutting down the number of lines he could handle making his resignation unavoidable — not at all calculated to start a hassle. However, the sales manager, sensing the evasion, and thinking to ferret out some devious, probably competitor-inspired scheme to do his company in, imperiously came back with an indignant demand for a better explanation. This is the response the rep would have *liked* to make:

Dear S___:

So you have to know, really, in all honesty you emphasize, why I resigned your line! You just don't understand it, you say. Well, all right — you asked for it.

You tell me your company makes excellent products (true), that your pricing is competitive (also quite correct), the commission rate is in line with others in the same category (Yup), so what more is necessary, you ask. Mister — that's exactly your problem! You just don't seem to realize that someone has to *sell* these things! Which is where guys like me come in. And, the reasons why I want *out*, in your case on what would otherwise be a desirable line, run like this:

1. You keep asking repeatedly for "feedback" (your favorite word, seems like!) until I am sent into howling oscillation every time you put it to me! I just can't continue being swamped with so many Mickey Mouse forms to fill out, with endless demands for trivia reports. My business is *selling*—not writing. I use my time to report—not only to you, but to all my principals—*if, as, and when I have something to say that will contribute information calculated to help our cause.* Why should I take time out from my work to write you reports proving I am working?!

2. Your company recently added *a new product* which, admittedly, appears promising. But you ought to know: a rep looks at a new number and asks himself: *is this something for a market that exists in my territory, or must a market be created for it?* The difference in the time, the kind and amount of effort required from the rep to sell it, is profound.
In this case, though an intriguing-looking device, its uses were yet unknown. The trade needed education on it from both the factory and the rep. You did no more from your end than to supply samples, to be followed by driving me nuts with repeated demands for orders—while we were out in the field sowing the seed, demonstrating and promoting the damned thing with a view to *building* a market for it—and, get this—working with money we earned *elsewhere*, hoping in time we might be compensated for our investment. Did you pay us anything by way of helping us pioneer the item? At least—since I was willing to put out my own money to promote it, why couldn't you have stayed off my back while I was trying to do my job?

3. You have been unreasonably insistent that we give

you *extended coverage beyond our regular territory* — that is, by making arrangements with reps in adjoining territories to sell your line, for me to split commissions with them. Baloney! That is a common way for brand new reps to get started — that is, taking on the lines of an established rep on a split commission basis and may be all very well for that newcomer. But so far as I am concerned, avoiding this entanglement is one of the hardway lessons I learned in the School of Life. To try and make you understand so that you may not bug some of your other reps with similar demands to do your marketing for you, I'll explain:

(a) If I appoint a sub-rep to handle your line, sooner or later his human nature comes to the fore. He figures he's doing all the work — why should he continue getting only a part of the commission? So we have potential for ill feeling and trouble. Or, if — supposing the line goes well, it could very likely lead him to taking on a competitive line, in order for it to be *his* line and so that he can receive 100% of the commission — and *our* line has helped him with a ready-made list of customers to whom he can go with *his* new line. What's the profit in that?

(b) If the principal is slow in paying commissions (which you *have* been at times), that would get me involved into making excuses and apologies for you, very possibly to result in arguments. Perhaps I would have to settle the matter by paying him out of my own pocket. Why should I buy such headaches?

(c) I have plenty to do working intensively in my own, well defined territory. Why should I have to undertake *your* marketing problems in covering areas nearby but outside of my regular operations? If it's a case of a state or territory being too big for one firm to cover, it's up to *you* to map out the territories and appoint reps to cover accordingly — that is one of the reasons marketing managers exist.

4. Again and again, I have had to beg for *reasonable supplies of literature* describing your products. Manufacturers who know their business put out appropriate quantities of catalogs, spec sheets, bulletins, envelope stuffers, price lists, keeping all printed matter up to date, but particularly supplying their reps with good quantities of literature for hand distribution and for mailing campaigns. But you — ! Well, Mister, I just got tired of hearing about the customers' unanswered requests for literature, and of their subsequent remarks reflecting on me, as though I was at fault in neglecting their requirements.

5. In the length of time it takes you *to get out a quotation*, I've had competitors quote, sample, and take the order — thereby wasting all the time and effort I put into getting the prospect interested. I've had to spend my money for followup phone calls to the factory, asking for answers to routine questions that could just as well have been taken care of in plenty of time by mail if you had tended to my queries promptly . . . I've had you arrive in town without a reasonable amount of notice, disrupting my agenda, making it necessary to drop everything in order to meet you at the airport and chauffeur you around, to call on customers you wanted to see . . . I've had you ignore my advice on how to approach customers whom I've known for years, to be followed by your blunders destroying their good will for me.

I've had it! I'm through with supplying the "how" for you, as in "how-to." Nor will I have to listen to any more of your snide remarks about the favor you do me in letting me rep your line. You must have cousins among those smug buyers who make condescending remarks about how rich I'm getting on the orders they give me!

There's more—but I think I've said enough, before I begin losing my temper.

Honest and truly,
Your erstwhile representative.

The foregoing "letter" was never written, of course, (although I have an idea there are reps who would like to do that!) As should be evident, it is a composite, a melange, a collection of sins to be laid at the doors, one by one, probably of many sales executives. But as a guide to reviewing his own relations with his reps, some sales managers just might discover objectionable characteristics or practices in themselves, which could explain some of the difficulties arising in dealing with independent representatives. Of course, to be honest with oneself, to see oneself as others see us . . . one can but try! □

8

TO LADY LIBBERS

An explanation

Being of the generation raised to believe that among the major functions of a man's existence was maintenance of a protective role insofar as women were concerned, I stare bewilderedly at the stalwart female of today in some of her strangely chosen occupations and avocations—as police officer, West Pointer, shotputter, utility pole climber, Little Leaguer, fire fighter, truck driver, to say nothing of such as the bone-breaking roller skater thing.

But aside from muscle-trying activities, it seems that here and there, women are getting into manufacturers' sales representation—that is, I'm referring not to working for a rep employer but as reps on their own. Well—I don't see a chasm comparable to the big biceps occupations between men and women when it comes to manufacturers' representation. Not at all: If they know what they're doing—

Of course, many are in conventional and, I would think, quite suitable occupations although I have found some women a bit remiss in the usual trade lingo and proper usage of products with which they become identified. Recently I was looking at an array of plastic shelf sets, each in a different color, on display in the bathroom fixture section of a department store. The young clerk who approached didn't look too much older than one of my granddaughters but she was very businesslike and quite the salesman—excuse—salesperson in pointing out how attractive they were. I agreed a set would be useful in my bathroom and said,

"I'll take the blue one."

"These are for display, sir. We have them in the back—uh —broken up—I'll put one together for you."

I smiled gently, trying not to sound condescending. "Don't you mean 'knocked down,' dear?"

"Oh? Is that the way—yes, I guess so." She didn't resent my correction but frowned, evidently trying to fix the expression in her mind. Leaving to get my selection, she returned within a few minutes to say, "I'm sorry, sir—we're all out of the blue ones—uh—knocked down. Would you mind taking one of those"—she pointed to the wall display— "that's knocked up? Of course it's a little dirty, but—"

"Yes, yes," interposed this grandpa hastily, to forestall further locutions. Thinking of myself as something of a good Samaritan, albeit with a dirty mind, I agreed without further parley to accept the blue one she had pointed out, despite its "condition."

But getting back to repping: if the lady is proficient in the good and bad features and the usages of the product lines for which she might seek representation appointments, if she is familiar with the competition and marketing conditions of the territory she expects to cover, if she knows comparative price structures, discount procedures and special allowance practices in the industry for which she would seek lines, if she has selling experience in various fields that would qualify her for approaching a prospective customer properly, if she is willing to forego a regular, dependable paycheck, if she can refrain from a discouraged "Oh, me!" when returning to the office after a long day of making calls to find piles of paper work still stacked up that must be taken care of before leaving for the day—if, if, and more ifs of independent manufacturers' representation, I believe that insofar as a rep's life is concerned, she has just as much right to choose that occupation as the lady who goes in for professional wrestling. Or painting church steeples. Or whatever.

So far as this writer is concerned, I have no comments to make on women's liberation other than to explain that despite philosophic acceptance of such modern-day practices as saying "salesperson" rather than "salesman," there are nevertheless points in this text where, despite my good intentions, habits of a lifetime have no doubt allowed "salesman" to be used where a lady libber might have preferred a neuter term.

Where that so happens, my apologies ladies — or should I think of you as "women" and not as ladies? Please forgive any transgressions this time. In the future, I'll try to keep in mind that things have changed from the days when "vive la difference" was the memorable outcry proclaiming a discovery comparable to finding the world was round instead of flat, when we looked consequently with pleasurable anticipation and zeal to exploring the hills and valleys of the — uh — world. □

9

ON MAKING A FORTUNE

— (or a reasonable facsimile thereof)

I don't know how many are reps but I read recently that in the mid-seventies, there were 215,000 millionaires in this country (and 215,000 million more trying to be one!). Which brings up the question — just what are the chances for a manufacturers' representative to get rich? Well — first — let's consider how it goes in other fields that are familiar.

In commenting on the new prevalence of nudity in the entertainment world, the incomparable Bob Hope remarked, "You don't have to take your clothes off to make money." And, *he* could very well prove it! That brings to mind the commentary of that cynic of a bygone generation, H. L. Mencken, who was fond of calling the country's citizens easy marks, of vowing there is no bottom to the gullibility of the American public. In other words: the one says to make money in this country, you don't *have* to exceed the bounds of propriety, and, by the same token, the other that it doesn't require an IQ rating of genius to make your mark from the marks.

Aside from the famous entertainer, there are many others who could "prove it." Although most trod traditional roads, there are those who acquire great wealth by bizarre processes, resulting from unlimited imagination. Some of these methods, while not necessarily illegal but surely outlandish, seem to bear Mencken out with a vengeance. Every day sees mounting evidence of people's willingness to buy damned near anything. One is induced to wonder why it should be at all difficult to make money — at least, enough enabling one to retire in decent comfort at a reasonably early age.

Of course, there are those who don't find having a lot of money necessary in order to be happy. I recall a strange chracter I met a good many years ago. I had returned to the garage where I occasionally parked. The manager who got my car out for me was a stocky fellow, heavy browed, with fiery dark eyes, deep-set in a rather darkly repelling visage, reminding me of the descriptions writers use in comparing their villains to the devil. He absently started to walk away, whistling some tune of the day, without collecting the usual parking fee.

"Hey!" I called after him. "No charge today?"

He returned and held out his hand saying, "Six bits." With a shrugging grin he added, "It's only money."

"Got all you want, eh?" I handed him three quarters.

"Correction — about all I need. I eat. I drink. I got a place to sleep — alone or with company if I want. After all — I've had my three greatest wishes in the world — who could ask for anything more?"

I was still smoking in those days. As I settled back in the driver's seat, I got out a cigarette and, complying with the usual smoker's etiquette, offered him the pack. He waved it away, pointing to his chest. "Gassed — in France — the war."

"Oh — sorry to hear that."

He laughed. "Hell's fire — that's how I got my first wish. Always wanted to see Paris. Used to dream about it. Well — I got there. They sent me back from where I'd got gassed in the trenches, to a hospital in Paris to recuperate — and did I see Paris! Wow!"

"And your second wish?"

"To diddle a Salvation Army lass."

I sat bolt upright. Unperturbed by my shocked expression, his eyes glistened with the memory and he grinned as though with some distant memory.

"You-you didn't—?" I gasped.

"Sure as hell did!"

"You bastard! How?'

"She was the one assigned to wheel me around the hospital grounds in my wheel chair every day, usually winding down a little path bordered by trees. I kept up the act of needing the chair going for a long time. One day, I got her to bring some sandwiches along for a kind of picnic instead of my regular lunch. We stopped back of some thick foliage and it was there—." He grinned, the lines in his face becoming deep crevices, making him appear more demoniac than ever.

"So what was your third wish—to assassinate the pope or something?"

"Nope. To walk on streets of gold."

"Not for you!" I stepped on the starter. "You'll never reach heaven! You'll burn in—"

"I did it! After the war, I wound up in Nevada—supposed to be best for my lungs. I came to a ghost town that had once been a roarin', hell-raisin' center back in the gold rush days. The prospectors had hit a rich vein. By way of celebrating, they decided to pave the town's only street. The day the surfacing was laid, those miners got crazy drunk and they sprinkled handsful of gold dust into the paving mixture. I meandered through the town, and that's where I walked on streets of gold!"

Well—with due allowance for exceptions like that one there, most men get their kicks out of more conventional achievement—usually like making money, and how big some people do it! Have you ever stopped to consider what fantastic sums are paid out by the public for products aimed at doing something about the perfectly normal secretions, excretions or exhudations of the human body? Like, in only one year, the public cheerfully shelled out something approaching three-quarters of a billion dollars for just one

company's cosmetics—lotions, potions and various intimate
body gimmicks—and that one not even the biggest of such
manufacturers. "Exhudations?" What is there to be said
about the multi-millions people expend just for dispersing
the normal odors emanating from armpits or the feminine
crotch—as promoted by revolting TV commercials that
would have you believe the use of soap and water has
become obsolete? Why take the trouble to bathe when, with
a squirt or two from a can—? And how about the three
hundred million a year for laxatives, those Roto Rooters of
the human body? Or the—

It takes big companies with big capital to get such results,
you say? Did they start "big" or did they begin in somebody's
kitchen, the garage or back of some guy's ears? Awright—
you want an instance of *one* individual's success all alone
with practically no investment? So what about the case of
some two million people paying out $4.00 each within a
couple of months for just plain, everyday rocks, purporting
to be household pets? Mencken would have said, "proves
my point"—snorting that there are people who must
already have the rocks, but in their heads!*

How about three-quarters of a *billion* in one year for
spaghetti sauce—just the sauce, for gosh sake? We won't
offend the sensibilities of true believers by referring to
those who make it in foretelling the futures with twaddles of
astrological terminology, to say nothing of raking in the
shekels by reading palms or tea leaves except that I
wouldn't be at all surprised to hear it has become popular to
have predictions of the future made by studying the locations of dandruff deposits on one's head!

---

* Another lone operator, although in this case a lawbreaker and certainly
not to be emulated, but worth noting in passing, was the case of that ad-
vertiser in national publications offering land on the moon at $4.95 per
acre, who actually received over 800 orders, many accompanied with the
money, before the postal authorities caught up with him!

Is it trite to say, what others have done, you can do? "Trite?" Would you prefer "Tripe"? Still believe it takes some unearthly brilliance to conjure up legitimate ways of making a lot of money? Tell me—what extraordinary outburst of brain power is needed to produce the scene in a TV show of a man in a hospital, awaiting news of the birth of his child, when the guy is presented as going bananas and making a gibbering fool of himself as the nervous father to be? Does someone need the talent of a Shakespeare to contrive such a side-splitting scene?

And speaking of that all pervasive television, how about the big money people are paid for those same old excitement-inducing, tire-squealing chases characteristic of the crime shows (often broken up by commercials for remedies offered to reduce the blood pressure their shows raise)? And consider that stroke of genius the TV people now resort to for replacing the cigarette break: now that the castigation of smoking prevents the actor from lighting up to halt the action, to portray a heavy thinking spell, say, along comes a great substitute, a diversion thought up by brains paid for with real money—namely, when the actor has to introduce a pause, his stall is to resort to a decanter of liquor on a handy table. Maybe I'm wrong but does every living room have to have bottles of liquor sitting out in the open like that, with a dish of ice (non-melting, of course) conveniently placed alongside?

Well—apparently we've wandered far afield from manufacturers' representation. Not so! While it may have its problems, the point is that the achievement of financial success need not be looked upon with too pessimistic an eye. Au contraire! We are surrounded with and part of the universe's continuing processes of creation; it is for each of us to get into orbit.

I ran across a very learned treatise recently, having to do with how industries start, grow and become obsolete, with new ones replacing them. The article claimed that to exist, to grow, to make it big, one should look for people's needs, reminiscent of what Paul Getty said, when asked how to become a millionaire, "Find a need and fill it." The article went on to decry the belief that an industry does not begin with a patent, a new device or new material developed.

Well—depends on how you look at it. Did electronics come along in answer to a "need"? Nylon? Cosmetics? Which comes first, the market or the product?

Suppose we agree that the canning industry grew because of a "need" to store perishable food. So? Certainly there are needs and products ostensibly intended to fill them. But also there are products that begin simply with an idea—who knows from where it came?—like the one for a labeling gadget useful in offices and households from which the labeling material itself is enough to establish a multi-million-dollar corporation. Within recent memory, there was the man starting from a fruit stand who became the ruler heading up a worldwide shipping empire, to take unto himself for a queen one of the world's most famous women. One could go on . . .

Ah, yes, but—perhaps, like this writer, your wants are quite modest. You'd like it but you don't need to become a millionaire? You already have a perfectly good wife whom you dearly love? You'd be satisfied with, say, just enough pelf to retire, to live comfortably, simply to be able to afford and enjoy some of life's more gracious offerings? Well, in that case you might think in terms of men who started up as manufacturers' sales representatives with one or two lines, grew, to ultimately build up enterprises doing business in the millions, employing staffs of two, or three, sometimes up to a dozen or twenty or more associates, advancing on the first million—oh—you've already started into that? Not that big, but—

So what's it all add up to? Simply this: America is still the country of free enterprise. What the many have done, others can do. The intent of this book is to offer a philosophy of thoughts, ideas, suggestions and methods calculated to help speed you on your way—for some to making a fortune but, at least, a reasonably satisfying facsimile thereof. How **much** you make—that's up to you. □

PART II

*"It's not nice to fool human nature —
but it pays to understand it"*

10

HAVE CONTRACT — WILL TRAVEL

Without that passport, you'd better stay home!

There are those people who have Faith — such as to say, that if one prays, the situation has been placed in the best of hands. Even agnostics allow for the helpful potentialities of a Higher Power.

I believe in prayer. I'm never through with thanking God for helping me out when He knew, as I had told Him, I had no one else to turn to. But if I enter into a sales representation agreement with a manufacturer that declares my remuneration is to be based solely on commission, I'm going to damned well make sure to get a *written*, mutually fair sales agreement. That is, I wouldn't want to bother God with this negotiation when He is so preoccupied with all the bombing and the pollution and the using up of the earth's natural resources and all the rest of the mess humanity has got itself into. It would be for us two parties to the deal (and my attorney) to work out.

I enjoy writing. I hope what I have to say is useful. There is one disheartening subject, however, of which I grow weary and would like to skip except that, as the very heart of the rep's existence, it is still not given sufficient consideration. It is subject to misplaced faith and capable of plunging the rep into disaster because it wasn't handled properly to begin with — and that is, the initial, formalized arrangement to represent a given manufacturer.

I suppose I shouldn't be sarcastic but I simply cannot understand how, with so much information available on the subject, with the frequently well publicized disastrous experiences that reps with contracts have suffered, with the prima facie need for just plain old common horse sense, it passes belief why there are still those sufficiently naive who take on representation based on no more than a letter of appointment or, even worse, only a phone call or a handshake.

If nothing else, how can one depend on an informal "understanding" with a sales manager humanly subject to becoming physically incapacitated or even passing away, who might perhaps switch to some other company himself or find himself fired in order to make way for the owner's nephew? So many, many things can happen to bring a third party into the agreement whose ideas of carrying it out may vary entirely from the rep's "understanding" of it. It takes a man with plenty of guts to go into repping, with all its risks and hard work, its sacrifices. In order not to have it all gone for naught, he would do well to be guided by those who bear the scars of experience when it comes to sales representation agreements.

At the time of negotiating the contract, it would have been no doubt in an atmosphere of optimism, with the newly joined principal and rep thinking favorably of each other, enthusiastically putting together a deal they felt was going to be mutually profitable. That their deal might some day change to a togethermess would be a remote thought, but such an unpleasant possibility is nevertheless one which is not to be overlooked by the alert professional, the one whom sad experience has taught to invoke safeguards against perhaps isolated instances but the not impossible likelihood of being screwed by some unscrupulous manufacturer.

Merely to have a contract is far from enough. If it isn't a good one, you might be better off without any at all. You could be blithely working away, under the euphoric impression that you have an arrangement which takes care of things, whereas there could be present or absent just one little provision or clause capable of making the agreement worth less than the paper it is written on if you hadn't taken the proper precautions at the time it was negotiated.

It so happens, just as I was working on this very chapter, I heard an attorney at a trade show relating a graphic case recently concluded which, as he said, never had any business hitting the courts and, I sighed, will they never learn? It was one more example of human nature in a very common situation :

At the time of negotiating the agreement, both parties were presumably concerned only with how great things were going to be.They signed a typical sales agreement, seemingly covering all the usual formalities. It included the all-important termination provision which the sales manager adamantly insisted must be limited to 30 days notice, to which, with much misgiving, the rep had finally agreed. Unfortunately, his mind was so occupied with the number of days notice specified in the event of termination, that he completely overlooked what was to happen *after* the 30 days of grace would be over with.

So, the arrangement had been in force for a couple of years, with the line moving along in pretty good shape, commissions paid as agreed — all seemed well. Then — a big order on which he had been working with all he had for almost a year, came through, to total something over a half million dollars! Commission rate was 7.5%. Excitedly, he phoned his principal the good news and was told, Swell, you're doing a great job, rush confirmation. With the order confirmed, the precious formal document forwarded to the factory, the rep visualizing the amount of commission he was to collect, jubilantly told his wife to call a travel agent to make arrangements for that long-dreamed-of European trip, about to become a reality.

Two weeks passed. One morning came the clamoring fire alarm that awoke him from his dream — in the form of a telegram. (A telegram is writing, isn't it? That was what the agreement had specified.) The message was from his principal notifying him that in accordance with their contract's provision, he was hereby given 30 days notice that his services would no longer be required after the expiration of that period.

Of course, a half-million-dollar order would take months in the preparation so that it couldn't possibly be shipped until long after the 30 days had passed. Now, hurriedly digging out the sales agreement, he pored through it word for word searching frantically for something which would specify commissions to be paid after termination on orders previously taken and still in the works. Nothing!

Not one word that would relate to the hereafter! He had overlooked omission from the paragraph that should have been a basic accompaniment to a termination condition. Though it specified, properly enough, that commissions would be paid in the month following shipments made in the previous month, that was where it stopped! Nothing was said about commissions to be paid on orders in the house, not yet shipped, *in the event the agreement was terminated!* And this manufacturer took full advantage of the rep's carelessness.

So now, at this late date, he consulted his attorney. They sued. How much of that rep's time was frittered away while sitting around in the attorney's office in the courtroom, biting his nails, preparing to testify on the witness stand! . . . The verdict was sad: what the decision came down to was that a contract is a contract, that after the 30 days were up, everything was over, relationship severed, finished, kaput forever . . . Well, the attorney managed to get it to a higher court where he did get the verdict reversed on the rather nebulous grounds that the manufacturer had violated what was fair to *both* parties in a contractual relationship . . . Heavy expenses had to be paid: the attorney got half of the final award, the trip to Europe went back to a dream status.

*　　　　*　　　　*

Incidentally, readers of my previous books have asked for the suggested ERA formula previously mentioned with regard to severance pay in the event of termination spelled out. With all thanks to ERA for setting up this very fair arrangement, here it is:

The amount to be considered as a base figure after termination would be the total of the previous year's commission. Each severance payment, due monthly, would be 1/12 of that total, as follows:

For the number of years representing the manufacturer		The number of payments to be:
From 2 years to	4 years max.	1
4	6	2
6	8	3
8	10	4
10	12	5
12	14	6
14	16	7
16	18	8
18	20	9
20	22	10
22	24	11
24	26	12

*　　　　*　　　　*

A tremendous rep vs. principal suit that received national notice, stemming from no commission paid after termination, offering the fact that the rep had to work for a good many *years* before a target order was landed, was decided in the rep's favor on the grounds of that which was *fair, even* though the contract had been terminated in accordance with the way it *read*. The commission involved ran in the hundreds of thousands of dollars.

There is a noticeable tendency for the courts to take into full consideration that which is "fair," as well as the actual wording of the written agreement. Aside from the specific provisions of the contract if, in correspondence, your principal says you will always get *fair* treatment, especially if in reference to possible termination, such can be most meaningful to the court in the event you get into a dispute reaching that far. But, don't count on it! The word "fair" has varying interpretations to different people!

*   *

A contract provision relating to another rather often bypassed subject is the clause which refers to the effect that within the territory specified, the rep should be commissioned on *all* business emanating from that territory. In a word, "exclusive." It should spell out that the rep is to receive his commission no matter how the order gets to the manufacturer — from the rep, direct from the customer, over the transom or from wherever. It should be worded to preclude the possibility of the manufacturer resorting to a claim that it wasn't the rep who produced the business but that it resulted from a manufacturer's advertising, a special visit from one of their factory men, a conversation with somebody or other at a trade show or a referral by slow boat from China. Regardless, unless specifically excluded in so many words in the written agreement, it should so state that the rep is to receive his full commission on *all business coming out of that territory*.

*   *   *

A comparatively recent subject for inclusion in the sales agreement is the matter of product liability protection. In the past, claims under guarantees or warranties, or damages originating from usage or failures of the product, and so on, were just tacitly for the manufacturer to worry about and take care of, not at all to be considered the rep's responsibility. Well, it's very different today. We have a multiplicity of new laws, of new bureaucratic agencies such as the Consumer Products Safety Commission along with its Nader-like consumer advocates, both individual and class action suits, all of which may very well include the manufacturers' sales representative in the distribution chain of responsibility. As a starter, the rep should have his attorney draw up a clause making it mandatory for the manufacturer to take unto himself all product liability, from the moment his product leaves the factory until it reaches the ultimate consumer—*and thereafter!*

Ask your prospective principal if he carries such protective insurance (he's crazy if he doesn't. Do you want to be affiliated with someone who's nuts?) and does he include his reps in his insurance? If he waves you off with a casual, "Oh, that's all taken care of," ask *how*. Specifically who *is* the insurer? . . . If you feel reluctant to ask such questions, just remember you have only one neck to extend for your principal—so don't be bashful!

*   *   *

If you are negotiating a sales agreement for a line on which considerable growth may be expected, it could be useful to set up a sales volume quota with a given basic commission but with an increasing rate as that volume figure increases. If this is specified in writing at the time of making the agreement, it could forestall much in the way of possible future dispute.

*   *   *

As is often set up in the case of the higher echelon employees of large corporations, you might try to negotiate a favorable arrangement for acquiring stock in the company you sign up with if you feel your services are going to be substantially effective in helping that manufacturers' stock to appreciate. It not only means money to you but helps give that feeling of being part of the family if you "own a piece of the rock"—which is mighty good for morale all-round.

*   *   *

A little tip: although used freely through this and other books, it is suggested that you avoid using the word "contract" when negotiating with a manufacturer. It has forboding significance—the legalize sound of it can frighten some. Preferably, say, "sales agreement," which comes to the same thing and should do fine in most respects.

*   *   *

What led to the actual placing of an order, might be very hard to trace in origin; the unquestioned majority of a territory's business stems from long, not necessarily visible, arduous ploughing of the field by the rep. Your sales agreement should look ahead on this point. And finally, to those readers of the foregoing who are sales managers or the equivalent thereof, who might take umbrage at the severe implications of the admonishments in the foregoing chapter: please understand that any veteran rep can recite instance after instance of manufacturers who took advantage of the fact that they didn't have to risk any direct investment in sales with guys around willing to work their heads off for that ephemeral "pie in the sky" commission check. Rep firms are small as compared to manufacturers as a rule, without staffs of attorneys at their beck and call, with little recourse from injury.

From your standpoint, Mr. Sales Manager, there should be no reluctance to *assure* fair play as asked for by the rep in the interests of what is only good business. After all, you have a built-in advantage—if you don't feel the rep is doing right by you, it is within your province to rid yourself of him at your option. For him, it's not that easy—hence the need for pre-assurance. Reasonable? ☐

11

ARBITRATION

The how-to stay out of litigation

"Hi, Bill. Good Convention, eh? How'r you doing?"

"Hi. Not so good. Just got a 'Dear John' letter."

"Oh — one of those. Too bad. Had the line long?"

"Two years. Just starting to be worthwhile. First year cost me plenty — promoting it, talking it up to the trade, special mailing campaigns — took lots of digging, you know? Didn't make postage stamp money. Second year, my pioneering started to bring results — orders coming in pretty good. I was looking forward to this third year — they had been making me all kinds of promises when blooey, in comes a new sales manager. This guy doesn't think our two-man operation is big enough for him — wants a multi-man company to rep His Majesty."

"He'll learn!"

"Yeah, but — in the meantime, I get notice and out. I ought to be paid at least 50% of the third year's commission and maybe fourth. I'm going to sue them."

"Got an arbitration clause in your contract? That would be so much better than time-consuming, costly litigation."

"H'm. Yes, seems to me there is something about arbitrating in the contract — but that's all it says. I guess I'd be willing, but what do you do? How do you go about it?"

"Meet me for lunch tomorrow — I'll have all the info for you."

"There are a great many problems that should not come to judges at all and can be disposed of in other ways — better

> *ways. I can suggest one basic way that must be developed more widely in this country and that is the use of private arbitration . . . Many lawyers, including the best lawyers in this country, press their clients in a great many business engagements between corporations to agree that all disputes between them will be resolved by private arbitration without any resort to courts and without any judicial review . . . We must use this highly acceptable device that in the long run is probably less expensive and at least as efficient and fair as any judicial process."*
>
> Chief Justice *WARREN E. BURGER*
> *From an interview published in Forbes Magazine*

Many sales agreements include a declaration that in the event of dispute between the principal and the sales representative, the matter will be submitted for arbitration. However, although arbitration intent in the event of serious differences *should* be included in *every* such contract, simply to *state* that it will be done isn't very good. That doesn't explain *who* the arbitrator will be, where, and if a dispute arises, how do you go about it and what does it cost. **Just what are the mechanics of arbitration?** What do you do to put it into effect? Who does it? In what ways is it superior to court action? Does it take as long as court proceedings? Is a lawyer necessary?

With the proliferation of modern-day litigation—disagreements between business entities, class actions, lawsuit piled upon lawsuit, the courts become all but inundated. Their enlarged caseload, forcing consequent interminable delays, with moneys tied up and time lost, can be disastrous to disputants over matters which could be settled expeditiously and fairly by other means.

Arbitration is a good answer.

Just what is arbitration? It is a legally binding alternative to the court system, whereby the two parties to a disagreement voluntarily submit their problem to a neutral third party for a decision. It is preferable that a clause agreeing to arbitration in the event of dispute be inserted in the contract at the time it is set up. Under the Rules of the American Arbitration Association (the largest neutral, non-profit administrator of arbitration hearings in the country), the parties themselves choose the arbitrator from a panel of qualified professionals. These arbitrators (who sit voluntarily as a service to their colleagues) listen to evidence from both parties in informal hearings, and then render an "award"—a decision in the case that is binding on both parties.

The advantages of arbitration should be obvious. First, the proceedings and awards are confidential—especially important in a case where one or both parties relies on reputation or public image. Second, the neutral arbitrator knows the field of the dispute, saving the parties a great amount of preliminary presentation time. Only the facts of the disagreement, and not general background information, have to be related during the hearing.

Third, arbitration is much faster than a court trial. Proceedings are less formal than litigation in court rooms, consequently the typical fine technicalities that lawyers raise, taking up so much time, are by-passed. With regional offices always nearby, consulting AAA for arbitration advice, submitting the disagreements, selecting the arbitrators and holding the hearings are procedures handled conveniently and with expedition.

Who is the American Arbitration Association? Founded in 1926, the AAA is an organization whose support comes from large foundations such as Ford, Rockefeller, Carnegie and others, from various industrial units, lawyers, nationally known manufacturers as contributing members and the nominal fee charged for its services. It numbers something on the order of 40,000 men and women giving their services without charge as arbitrators, a panel selected from lawyers, engineers, architects, bankers, including a huge number of specializing categories, each one chosen for expertise in a given field. In its fifty years of existence, among its twenty-one regional offices located all over the country in well known cities, the AAA has administeredf as many as 35,000 matters in a year.

A broad range of services in addition to private commercial arbitration and mediation is offered, such as mediating and conciliating labor disputes, handling medical malpractice claims through arbitration, issuing a stream of literature, films, scholarly publications — and digests of current court decisions on arbitration. It is a logical resource in the creation of impartial systems for taking such disputes out of the court through the use of contractual systems of dispute settlement.

What do you do to use AAA? Assuming you and your principal are agreed on arbitration: when you include in your agreement an arbitration clause naming the AAA, you rely on AAA service and you place upon the AAA the responsibility of providing that service. You will enable AAA to carry out that responsibility with maximum speed and efficiency if you *advise the Association immediately when such a clause is used*, and not wait until a dispute arises to inform it of its responsibility.

The following clauses for insertion in commercial contracts are often used.Some parties will have particular needs that will require appropriate changes:

FOR THE
ARBITRATION OF
FUTURE DISPUTES:
          STANDARD ARBITRATION CLAUSE
          Any controversy or claim arising out of or relating to this contract, or the breach thereof, shall

be settled by arbitration in accordance with the
Rules of the American Arbitration Association,
and judgment upon the award rendered by the
Arbitrator(s) may be entered in any court having
jurisdiction thereof.

FOR THE
SUBMISSION OF
EXISTING DISPUTES:

We, the undersigned parties, hereby agree to
submit to arbitration under the Commercial Arbitration Rules of the American Arbitration
Association the following controversy (cite briefly). We further agree that the above controversy
may be submitted to (one) (three) Arbitrators
selected from the panels of the American Arbitration Association. We further agree that we
will faithfully observe this agreement and the
Rules and that we will abide by and perform any
award rendered by the Arbitrator(s) and that a
judgment of the Court having jurisdiction may
be entered upon the award.

The AAA Rules spell out the operation; just how the
Arbitrator is appointed, the procedures that then take place,
the hearings (at which you may present your own case or
have your attorney do it — your option). the manner of making the award — all the details of the entire arbitration
process. A copy of the "Commercial Arbitration Rules" and
other literature describing the Association's functions,
methods and its advantages is available upon request.
Address:

THE AMERICAN ARBITRATION ASSOCIATION
140 West 51st St., New York, N.Y. 10020

In the event of a dispute, when you have the arbitration clause in your contract, you write to AAA giving them your story or, perhaps preferably, just a summary of the highlights, and requesting their applicable forms. These you fill out, forward to AAA, and that gets the ball rolling immediately; no long, interminable waits such as you have to endure if taking the matter to court.

The Association's fees are quite nominal. They are based on the amount of the claim as disclosed when the claim is filed:

Amount of Claim	Fee
Up to $10,000	3% (minimum $100)
$10,000 to $25,000	$300, plus 2% of excess over $10,000
$25,000 to $100,000	$600, plus 1% of excess over $25,000
$100,000 to $200,000	$1,350, plus ½% of excess over $100,000

The fee for claims in excess of $200,000 should be discussed with AAA in advance of filing. When no amount can be stated at the time of filing, the administration fee is $200, subject to adjustment in accordance with the above schedule as soon as an amount can be disclosed. If there are more than two parties represented in the arbitration, an additional 10% initiation fee will be due for each additional represented party.   □

12

WAYS TO GROW

Some selected methods and comments

A newly formed association of independent sales representatives drawn from often-associated industries (plastics, electronics, hardware, automotive) had invited me to speak at
one of their meetings. Not being too sure of the group's
degree of sophistication, following the introduction I suggested we launch right into a question and answer period.

They turned out to be enthusiastic, alert, full of challeng-
ing questions. Finally, one of the younger men came up
with a dilly. It became the basis for discussion through the
rest of the evening.

"Do you believe manufacturers' representation still holds
good promise for a man?" he asked. "Would you go into it
under today's conditions if you were an unknown?"

"So much so," I replied, "that if I weren't otherwise involved, I'd start up tomorrow."

"Are there any moves in *particular* you would single out as
the most helpful in speeding up the solid establishment of a
new sales agency?"

"That's quite a question," I acknowledged. "I'm not going
to say that these are 'the most,' but I feel there are certain
procedures which I don't think receive the degree of con-
structive attention they deserve from the average rep—not
only the beginner, but many who have been long established. Old timers could well review them.

"One has to do with where and how one solicits lines. I'm
thinking of a source ordinarily passed by, and that is the
manufacturer who employes salaried salesmen rather than

using commission representatives. He is open and promising territory.

"Secondly, there is the poor use the average rep generally makes — if at all — of what can be a most powerful adjunct of business, particularly when in need of more manpower, and that is mailings to the trade.

"Thirdly, there are still too many, notably newcomers, who fail to realize how valuable it is to be a member of a trade association. I would join up at the earliest opportunity.

"And Fourth: I would cultivate the art of flattery — that is, as a selling tool. I might even go to the extent of taking special courses in applied psychology by way of helping to use that art properly. If my advanced years have given me any wisdom at all, it is to now realize that the hard way of life becomes so much smoother when lubricated by the oil of flattery."

Following is a recap of the suggested "moves" which occupied us in a lively discussion that went on until midnight.

I

SOLICITING DIRECT LINES — OPEN TERRITORY

I would search out the manufacturer in my product category still using directly employed salesmen, prompted by a straightforward, sincere belief that he would do better by adopting the independent sales agent system in marketing. If you don't already know of some such possibilities, a two- or three-step series of enquiries will lead you to them. As follows:

You start among the many people you know: who can they suggest who now sell "direct" but whose products lend themselves to handling by independent reps? How about those whom you are already calling on; from which manufacturers are they buying who employ direct factory salesmen? You continue with others. They may or may not be able to name such manufacturers. But if not, they will probably be able to suggest names of men in a position to refer you to such possibilities, whom you contact. You keep asking. You get more names; you are referred to still others. By the time you have reached the third "step," you will in all probability have a substantial list of sales managers who become your targets.

No doubt one of the first thoughts in connection with taking over "direct lines" by independent sales agents is the possibility of manufacturers getting the commission reps to build up territories for them and then, when the commissions become high, revert to putting in their own offices, with salaried men replacing their reps. Well, it would be stupid to deny that some manufacturers have done just exactly that—as their mistreated representatives have bitterly publicized. But what does not receive equal attention, somehow, is the fact that most of the turncoat manufacturers who replaced their reps with salaried salesmen, learned how mistaken they were to make that change and have quietly reverted to the commission rep system. They found their sales volume, that had gone down when they dropped the reps, went back up when returning to the independent representative system.

Incidentally, this is a good test of your selling ability. Keep in mind that a surprising number of manufacturers, even to this day, for outmoded or unthinking reasons, fail to realize the advantages of using the independent representative in the marketing of their products, perhaps even don't understand how it works. You have a wealth of persuasive material to draw on. There are so many valid points you can make.

Many a manufacturer nowadays turns out a wide variety of products, intended for differing markets. Start by showing him how professional sales firms vary in the market categories they work—some narrowly specializing but others ranging widely in their activities. The sales manager has an extensive range of choices to fit his coverage requirements among the independents. These marketing firms call on retailers, wholesalers, specializing or general line distributors, variety stores, manufacturers, research laboratories, government agencies and others; there are reps who concentrate on selling finished products, components, complete equipments or systems, covering all or selected divisions of such trade. In short, he has plenty to choose from.

Another point to bring out is that the independent rep is more suitable for the manufacturer when it comes to exploring potential business in outlying districts because, having a number of lines, costs of pioneering can be apportioned among them, which otherwise would be too costly a procedure for a salaried man. Then, too, the rep already knows the potential trade, is probably selling them one or more of his lines and therefore has easier access in bringing before the buyer still another line. Perhaps even more important: if you present your case properly, the sales manager will sense the enthusiasm of the self-employed, happy in the knowledge that he is building his own business as contrasted to the lackadaisical salaried salesman to whom the day's work is "only a job." Everybody knows enthusiasm is high octane when it comes to selling.

For such reasons, manufacturers once sold on using the independent sales rep, seldom revert anachronistically to the old direct salesman method of marketing. Surely, if a rep is bringing in a good volume of business, does it make sense to endanger that success by changing to a salaried man? Just as an immediate example of what I mean: I'm sorry names can't be mentioned but this writer happens to know right now of a firm representing one of the country's well known manufacturers, who has been doing a twenty-five to thirty million dollars annual volume for one manufacturer on a commission basis, whose contract was just unhesitatingly renewed this year, with no question of the principal changing to a factory direct selling office. All in all, one has to conclude that the cynical cracks about manufacturers reverting to direct salesmen are only seldom justified nowadays.

But in initially soliciting the line of a sales manager using direct selling people, you especially have to impress him with the fact of being a knowledgeable man, giving evidence of not only how familiar you are with your own local trade but with the industry in general. Since you are being looked upon as a *business man*, as much an *executive* as a cold turkey salesman, it is expected that your grasp of ambient conditions should be broad. Fine points, beyond self-evident or major qualifications, have considerable influence in making his decision.

The size of various companies operating in your territory's industry as roughly indicated by the number of employees is meaningful to the manufacturer, particularly in showing up market potentialities per company — data which is not too difficult for you to obtain. Helpful in the interview are references to trade's various practices, the dollar amount of the area's purchases, quantities, kinds of products they buy; familiarity with such background facts portrays the image of one who knows what is happening in that portion of the world which you call *your* territory.

Outside of your normal calls and activities, for gathering much varied information concerning the activities of the various companies in the territory, their past years' success and failures, their future plans and so on, educate yourself by studying the periodical stockholder reports issued by incorporated companies, contact financial/business editors of your local newspaper, your stock broker, and, especially discuss such subjects with your banker. (Invite the money man to lunch. He'll accept! Today's bankers are different — they've changed from high hat, frock coat to shirt sleeves, overlooking no opportunity to build good will. In any event, he's a good man to know).

Don't overlook *buyers outside of your own trade divisions* — in

fact, *anybody* who can add to your store of knowledge about
what goes on in your territory, who can supply tid-bits of
information to stow away in your memory banks, available
to play back during your interview and calculated to help
support your claim of being an authority on your territory —
in depth! — to thereby make you so much more impressive
to the interviewing listener.

Above all, and in a word: *actually* knowing your territory
in depth is not only influential in obtaining good lines but
has much to do with helping you to make good in results
after you get the line.

*What I have indicated in the foregoing envisions one helluva lot
of work, doesn't it? Yup, I agree! Sure is! Outside of getting yourself
born to wealth, sorry, I don't know any ways to get rich legitimately
without working hard for it!*

II

MAILINGS — WHY AND HOW

Mailings should loom up high in the promotion procedure
of any sales firm, new or old. Due to manpower limitations,
your sales volume may be only peanuts. (By no means said
lightly. One tends to be respectful of an industry which even
in the 1974 recession year still managed to run to two-and-a-
half billion dollars, to say nothing of producing a president
of the United States! Good use of the mails has the effect of
increasing your manpower because of its minor costs as
compared to calls in person. Not only that, but deeper
market penetration is effected. I've heard people perfunctorily admit: Yeh, making mailings is okay — while following
with excuses for passing up this method of helping to build
one's business. They'll plead lack of time or that they've tried
it without getting good results, that responses came from

time wasters, that postage rates are out of sight — etc.

Bull-bleep!

Usually the first plaint is difficulty in acquiring a good mailing list. Which really is not an insurmountable problem. There are a variety of sources, starting with the firms in the business of supplying such lists for every kind of classification you might think of. Naturally, they vary in quality. One source usually dependable is the trade publication.

Not all, but some trade publications offer arrangements for using their subscription lists, usually at a charge of so much per name. There are those who make an extensive deal of this, with lists of business entities broken down in categories such as manufacturing, financial, engineering, purchasing, etc. By computer selection, names can be supplied specifically for a selected geographical area, with individuals addressed to their place of business or home. Such selections are quite dependable for accuracy, being taken from their subscription lists.

Rosters of trade association members can be very productive. Such members are apt to be the most progresssive people in their particular occupations, aware of the value of cooperating with fellow members and likewise affluent enough to be able to pay the dues. The organizations may be made up of manufacturers, distributors, procurement officers, engineering societies, reps like yourself, and so on — but they are all buyers of something, whether it be sporting goods equipment, automotive items, air conditioning and who knows what-all, products among which there are bound to be some you sell.

If you don't know offhand of trade associations existing whose members might be prospective customers, your local library will have at least some of such groups' publications, and you can also obtain there the names of firms engaged in selling lists of such organizations.

Many firms exist who sell lists of names for mailing

purposes, varying from excellent to all but worthless. The better ones keep their lists fairly current, so that no more than a 3% to 5% error factor should be reasonably expected. However, good judgment must be applied in selecting the firm from which you obtain your list. Don't assume because the name of that supplier is nationally well known, you need no more assurance of the list's worth. I have seen an astonishing list supplied by one of the most famous national organizations in the country that was "loaded" — that is, large numbers of names were utterly useless, the addresses being wrong, the names unknown at the addresses given, envelopes stamped "no such street," mailings in many cases actually returned marked "deceased."

If contacting a firm selling mailing lists, request a sample covering the area in which you operate. In that case, you would doubtlessly recognize names shown or note those absent which you think might have been included, thus giving you a pretty good idea of what to expect from the complete list. Or, a good bet for checking the list out is to pay for a comparatively small number of names and make a test mailing with that sample. It would teach you much about the value of the names supplied — both as to name accuracy and kind of response you might expect from a major mailing of the same material.

So obvious that many people overlook it, but the "yellow pages" of the phone book offer a prolific source for your prospect list — names and addresses, with occupation neatly categorized for your purposes . . . Another excellent source (also mentioned in another connection) is when exhibiting at "Shows." Instead of blindly handing out literature and hoping it will do some good, refrain from having catalogs, etc. available at the booth. Instead, meet the requests for literature by having the people attending give you their names and addresses on your promise to have your office mail them the referenced literature. This provides a great opportunity to add good names to your list, as you study the people in person for your future guidance.

It may be that your trade association has a list of the territory's customers, or might be persuaded to compile such a list for the common usage of the members . . . An outstanding source would be the trade association directories in the categories of industry in which you are interested. Such members are usually the enterprising and responsible people in their trade divisions and consequently their names make up a quality list. . . . Purchasing agents usually band together. For them to have an active association is quite common and, if you can get their roster, you would have a list of inestimable value.

And of course, probably best of all, you may already have a good list to be compiled from your past activities, from bingo cards and other various inquiries made by prospective customers.

A valid objection to mailing campaigns but one which is given undue importance is the patent fact that postage costs have increased tremendously. True, of course. The days when you could mail a letter for three cents is a footnote in history and as for the penny postcard, it has become a collector's item. So? What is *your* income as compared to the days of your father's?

In any event—when you compare a letter with the cost of a sales call, expenditures for mailings become nominal. We're talking about a call on a prospect costing as much as eighty dollars. No? Fifty? Or, if the manner in which your costs of doing business are calculated by methods used B.C. (Before Coolidge) and you believe you can still make calls for thirty bucks or, with even fuzzier once-upon-a-time thinking, at fifteen dollars—

So—how many times have you made calls *without* getting an order? How many times can you afford (even at fifteen bucks per) to make non-productive calls? But suppose you have a mailing campaign going, to supplement your personal calls, going out several times a year. Smart reps make it once a month — in some cases even more frequently. How much would *that* cost — as compared to calls in person?

Okay, okay — granted — unless you are actually in some regular form of a direct mail order business, your mailings may not necessarily produce orders, per se. But — consider your mailing as a formal, inexpensive *call* on the prospect — *which is what it is* — the purpose being that of a *preliminary* sales talk, to soften up the prospect so that when you follow with a personal call, you're more apt to walk out with an order instead of even perhaps having difficulty getting in, plus the fact that you bring down the unit cost per order. It is a means of giving your territory extended coverage which might not otherwise be possible without additional manpower.

I would *not* go in for automated methods of setting up and maintaining a mailing list *at first*. In one way or another, as you gain experience in the uses of the mail in your business, *you will make many changes as you go along*. Don't lock yourelf in — don't be tempted into buying the fancy, impressive equipment offered for such purposes. Take your time! Get along as best you can with home brew methods, keeping in mind that you *will* eventually adopt automated methods but you will then be doing it from the standpoint of experience in grinding out mailings. You will then have acquired the expertise in knowing what you should have. I can guarantee that you *will* find reason to switch from whatever system you start with, so don't bury your money in something you are bound to discard sooner or later.

One word more along those lines: don't tie up your office personnel with the stuffing, sealing and stamping chore of getting out sizable mailings. It interferes with current business, it's tedious work, discouraging, and consequently likely to be put off too long — or altogether! It's poor economics. Turn the job over to one of the letter shops in your area set up for that kind of work — there are plenty of them. In the long run, it will pay you to thus farm your mailings out.

Let's assume you've acquired what would seem to be a pretty good list of names to begin with, but you haven't proved it out. You don't know how productive (or otherwise) your list may be. One way is to work up a **concise** letter, starting with whatever salutation is most appropriate in your industry (Dear Sir . . . Ms. . . . Gentlemen . . . Dear Friend . . . etc.) If you're new to the territory, in your opening paragraph state *briefly* you have opened a manufacturers' sales representation office to serve the trade of your area, including in what trade classification you operate. (If you're long established, just start with a *short* referral to how long you've been serving the trade in your area).

(I just stopped typing long enough to re-read the previous paragraph. Noting my preoccupation with the need for keeping that letter short, takes me back a long ways.)

During the years I was a radio distributor in Hollywood, I heard some outlandish, all but incredible stories — yet, there were those that actually happened. My stressing of brevity recalls the one told me by a veteran movie actor friend, which he swore was absolutely true. It had to do with a famous New York playwright, induced by a well known producer to come out to Hollywood on a deal including all expenses paid and a weekly stipend that was very big indeed. He was to do the script for a movie to be made from his current Broadway play.

The writer found himself ensconced in a luxurious Beverly Hills hotel-apartment, well stocked with fine liquors, rent paid and told to go to it. The first week, bringing his preliminary notes, he appeared at the studio intending to discuss his ideas with the producer. He was directed to an office window where his first, fancy check awaited him, but the producer was not available.

He returned to his lush abode to find a gorgeous blonde

waiting, who introduced herself as a secretary assigned to help him in any way possible. He thought of his wife back in New York, faithfully taking care of the children. A bit regretfully, but firmly, he told the gal he wouldn't need her. Expanding his notes to an outline, he came to the studio a second time, with the same result — the producer was "too busy" to see him but had left word for him to go right ahead. He picked up his check and went back to work. Settling down now to writing the full script, that routine was repeated each week — the check was always there but the producer was unable to see him. This went on until after six months, he had completed a fully detailed, ready-to-shoot manuscript. It made up a volume almost four inches thick.

This time, word having got through that the work was completed, the producer sent for him. Entering the plush office, the author introduced himself and handed the script over. Without opening it, the producer hefted it in his hand, screwed down his eyebrows in a thoughtful expression, hefted the script some more and said, "Twenty minutes too long!," handing it back to the stunned playwright with a dismissing gesture. When that still flabbergasted author appeared at the usual window the next day, instead of a check, the envelope contained a ticket for his return trip to New York.

Well, now that I've got that off the typewriter, let's get back to *your* short letter. Start with, "We will be offering — " (name of your product) accompanied with a very few quick descriptive adjectives, such as "the famous So-and-so" brand, the "Internationally renowned," the "country's favorite" — etc.,

Then go on with this thrust, perhaps underlined or in italics:

"We intend to be mailing you important announcements, informative literature, the latest catalogs, price list revisions, announcements of new products, competitive price news and various other items of special interest, to help keep you informed about trade developments. (If you would rather *not* receive such mail, we will respect your wishes — you have only so to indicate on the enclosed card — we'll pay the postage).

"Please take just one moment to check the postage-paid reply card enclosed — and drop it in the mail — today, please?

"Thank you. We're looking forward to being of service to you.

> "Cordially,
> "Joe Repper Company,
> "by_____"

To help get the largest possible number of returns on this, you might consider adding something on this order, as a postscript:

"P.S. If we receive your response by ____(date), we'll appreciate your cooperation by sending you ____." Here you describe a giveaway; calendars are pretty staple for this purpose but if only nondescript, not much of an inducement. Something not so common could be a slide chart or a plastic slide-rule calculator giving the kind of figures used in your business, cross-referencing fractional with metric figures. I've seen these advertised for around 60¢ or so. Or, you might offer a pen of better than ordinary quality, an imprinted desk pad, and so on.

Kept simple, that bounce-back card can be of tremendous value. It should read something like this:

Dear Joe: Date_____

Okay to retain my name on your mailing list?_____

Products in which I might be interested are _____

If salesman may call, best time? _____

Any special comments which might help us to serve you?

_____

Name _____ Company _____

Address_____ Dept. or Bldg. No. _____

Phone (____) ____ _____

Try the foregoing first with only a sample mailing, which might prove up some desirable changes before going into a very big mailing. In any event, such a short, simply worded letter, quickly to the point, with the indicated card enclosed:

1. Will help weed out the poorest names on your list.
2. Such a card returned and filled out, would give you un-questionably definite prospects on whom you can con-centrate both future mailings and calls in person, as cir-cumstances may indicate.

A couple of words more on mailing campaigns: don't try to economize on especially that first letter: it's initial impres-sions that can heavily influence your future relations with the addressees. Turn the printing over to a high grade craftsman, one whose work you have seen and admire. Whether it's cheaply or handsomely done, the person receiving your mail *will* unconsciously, if not directly, feel the quality of your letter and you get classified in his mind right then and there. (A point which goes for all your printed material, for that matter.)

III

TRADE ASSOCIATIONS—WHY BELONG?

At absolutely the earliest possible moment, I would be-come a member of a good trade association or whatever organization there is in your industry that corresponds to that general term. I have written at length elsewhere about the advantages of such affiliation—of being listed in direc-tories distributed among the trade, of enhanced status in the industry, of group rates on insurance, on miscellaneous purchases, on traveling, on car rentals, special hotel rates and so many other benefits.

A point not ordinarily brought out is that the new rep takes on a presumptive reputation for responsibility, of distinction from the hoi-polloi, just by virtue of membership in a well known trade group. It is short-sighted — in fact, I am constrained to say, out-and-out stupid — to assume that such organizations are only beneficial for the so-called "big" reps, those who are widely known in industry activities. As a matter of fact, the very size and prominence of the heavies obviates the real necessity for them of belonging to a trade association — they could go on their own power. It's the smaller firms who really benefit *more* because the big fellows are so well known that the newcomer, simply by being identified as one of their group, shares in the acclaim — he, too, must be somebody!

Another example of shallow thinking arises when a rep refuses to join a trade association with a snorting, "That outfit? It's run by a clique — always the same guys. They get all the publicity, the pat on the back. They're the ones who get all the credit for putting on the projects, the special events, and everybody gives them the big hooray. Why should I pay dues just to promote that gang?"

Talk about your cheap shots! Having often been a member of just such a so-called "clique" and consequently a target of such bullshots, I could only gnash my teeth down to the gums and look for a place to throw up. If that stupe only knew! Sure, the same old members are the ones apt to be carrying on the chores of the association — the "same" only because other members hang back, evade, and leave it to the volunteers, to those who are always *willing* to perform the necessary work!

It is only the "same" gang because of members who, when asked to serve on committees or in officerships, hurriedly refuse in one way or another, pledging how busy they are, how short-handed, haven't enough time to take care of their own business let alone the affairs of the association — and all that there clap-trap! Fortunate indeed is the organization with enough of such willing workers — they're the ones who carry the rest.

Yes, indeed — if I were starting again, I'd very quickly join up. I'd make myself heard. I'd take part in every possible activity of the association. If I weren't asked, I'd volunteer my services. Because —

I know it's rewarding! Remember the one about casting your bread upon the water and how it comes back a thousandfold? Meaning — the "bread" being the kind you take to the bank? Oh. Well, yes — sometimes. Could very well be. But nothing — no way — *nothing* beats the great, warming satisfaction of having done one's proper part in the commonality of one's fellow man. That reward is bread for the soul!

IV

FLATTERY — A TOOL FOR THE SKILLED

Flattery! Now here is one on which I am out in left field. I know the practice. I am familiar with just how it is used but I just was unable to employ it myself *ordinarily* — though with certain exeptions. Not because of any valid objections, mind you. I am fully aware that it is one of the most effective tools in the salesman's bag. Skillfully employed, it has been known to bring outstanding results. But we are all different. That's why we choose manufacturer's representation as an occupation for our individualism.

In my own case, I'm rather notorious for being a blunt, outspoken person, never hesitating to call them as I see them. Coming from me, flattery would not be in keeping; most people would readily recognize it for what it is and laugh in my face. That is why, as I said before, if I were to go into repping today, I would take up a course in psychology aimed at acquiring the techniques of this form to aid in selling presentations.

However, since it *is* one form of selling, and inasmuch as it can be, legitimately, a most effective tool, I am going to give it some discourse here. Whether or not to use flattery in your presentations is up to you — your judgment in this connection is as good as anybody's — probably better.

I think it's pointless to be captious about the ethics, say, of a salesman using blarney to influence a decision in his favor. Insincerity? F'r instance, why does one wear specially selected clothes, watching carefully not to say anything that will spoil the favorable impression we're trying to make? By the same token, is it objectionable to use certain words intended to add to that good impression, like expressing admiration for a buyer's qualities — whether they're real or imaginary?

The shotgun of flattery is known to be effective in shooting holes through the armor of the toughest prospect, thus making one way for the salesman to get through to him. That's when you're telling him you agree wi th his appraisal of himself, that he is great, or efficient, or smart, or talented, or has superior tastes or, in short, in one department or another, he is outstanding in your estimation.

Having established for yourself the fact that you are a man of discernment, possessed of good judgment (as your admiring words have shown!), it pretty much follows (says your subject's subconscious) that what you have to say about your *products* must likewise be pretty accurate since you have proved yourself to be one who knows what he is talking about.

Are most people too smart to be taken in by flattery? How about the famous entertainers in the TV talk shows? Notice how, no matter how many years of adulation they have had, let someone say something complimentary about him or her and, though superficially disclaiming praise, it is pretty plain that they like it — and for that matter, who doesn't? It serves a purpose — it helps put them at ease, makes them more responsive to the show's host who is *selling* — in this case his product is entertainment, that is.

Of course, as in my case, if you're not good at it, just to slop

it on like with a broom, *forget it*! Flattery is an art that calls
for discrimination in your selectivity of the subject, a glib
tongue, tactful timing, above all for subtlety within the conversation. For example: let's say your product is a mechanical device. The one I've heard (and secretly admired) the
way some men do it is, they say to the prospect "My,
my — it's a relief to be able to show this (name the product) to
someone like you — who's capable of understanding it. It's
so difficult for some people to get the point of how — " and
thus he goes on making his points while the prospect pays
close attention in order to justify being considered one who
is "capable of understanding."

Something might occur to interrupt the sales talk — a
phone call that the prospect has to answer f'r instance, an
employee breaking in with a problem, say. The flatterer
considers this a good opportunity. When he finally turns
back to the   rep, the latter resumes with, "Mr. Big, I've
noticed whenever I come in here that, in spite of always
being so busy, and having so many things to think about,
and being under constant tension — nevertheless, you always
seem to be so full of pep — you stay right in there — you don't
seem to get tired or lose your cool. I envy you — how do you
you do it?"

He may reply that it's his jogging five miles every
morning and he flexes his muscles, or that maybe it's the
good whiskey he drinks, or something else on that order — or
he may just smile at the complimentary words, but one can
bet *they will have been heard and found pleasing* — instilling an
attitude that helps make him respond favorably to the
sales presentation. . . . But — to be effective, you have to be
smooth at it!

Flattery and the big shot complex: Now here we have a whole
other thing. In this case, you can bring out the broom! I'm
speaking of contending with the galling kind of buyer who
feels enthroned, royally cloaked in the authority conferred

upon him, who imperiously fixes the salesman with an ominous scowl. He acts as though you are expected to salute, bow from the waist or bang, bang, you're dead. Yes, indeed yes—one is too often confronted with such Mickey-Mouse minds whose posturing display of authority is reminiscent of children at play. Vanity of the immature? Inferiority complex? Yup—probably both them things.

Talk about vanity! Brings back memories of a side-splitting business call I once made on a well known Hollywood personality—a woman who, as I sat in the visitor's chair, could only be seen from the chest up behind a huge desk. At first, I didn't know why I felt oddly uncomfortable, being an inch or two over six feet, to have to look up as I addressed the seated lady because, from what I could see of her, she just didn't seem to be a woman who would really stand unusually tall. At an early point in our conversation, she did have to get up in order to reach a file in back of her—and with that I got the picture. It was only with the greatest of difficulty that I restrained the guffaw struggling to escape me.

I now saw that the unusual dimensions of the desk were no illusion. It had evidently been especially paneled to conceal a platform built about ten or twelve inches above the floor so that, when this woman sat at the desk as one normally does, she could look *down* on her visitors. Actually, when she stood up, I saw that she was a bit short, about five feet tall I would guess—a dumpy figure, but not at all freakish—her build, that is! Oh, me!

The executive with the general-of-the-army complex, barking orders, throwing his weight around, has been pretty much retired from the modern business scene. But the one we still have with us is the underling, the "hired hand" who can make or break you with his authority to interview salesmen and to place the company's orders accordingly. There are those in this category who find it necessary to talk loud, to bluster, go out of their way to impress you with their importance. In lording it over the suppliers, he can be most detrimental to his employers and a crack in the glass to the vendors who have to call on him . . . Unfortunately, your success with the company employing him is at the mercy of this character. What do you do?

Well, flatter him! Pile it on! You not only overlook his guff, but you *agree* with him. Let him know you consider he is as big a man as he purports to be. If anything, go him one or two better. Examples—like this:

"I'm glad you're the buyer here, Mr. Big—it makes my job so much easier when I can talk to a man of (intelligence) (experience) (understanding) (patience) (fast at grasping details) (know-how) (ability) (such a perceptive person), etc." In his efforts to live up to your good opinion of him, he will become much more amenable to the features of what you are selling.

A good many years ago, I had my first encounter with the value of flattery as exemplified by a lady friend of mine, one with whom I occasionally had a very pleasurable date. Despite no great visible attractions, she was extremely popular with the opposite sex. She was quite thin, her nose had an odd upturn, but she did have a pleasing smile, with sometimes a glint of promise in her rather widespread eyes. I was quite mad about her.

When I say I saw her "occasionally" it was because that girl was almost always busy dating other men. One time I asked her, "In this line of guys always at your door, where do I stand?"

"Why you're the head man, of course," she smiled, "if there is such a thing as a line. Oh, of course, I do have a number of gentlemen friends. Just average guys. Any girl can have them by the bunch, you know—men are so vain. Of course, a fellow like you, you're too intelligent to fall for a lot of that stuff but you take so many men, all you have to do is tell them how good they are at this or that and, oh boy, how they go for it."

"Yeh," I grinned, adjusting my bow tie. "You are so right." I was feeling increasingly better over having squandered almost a week's pay on candy and flowers along with the tickets for the popular play we were going to attend that night. "Most guys think they're good."

The phone rang. I heard her tell the caller that she was busy tonight but "Friday would be just fine." She returned to apologize for the interruption. "He's a pretty nice person. Not a good conversationalist like you but, just for a change, to go dancing sometime—he's a pro you know."

"Yeh," agreed the good conversationalist. "Everybody's different, I suppose."

I was transferred to another city shortly thereafter. She wasn't very good at keeping up correspondence. Too busy, I assumed—with such as dancers and other "average men." Ultimately, my interests turned elsewhere and I lost track of her. Today—a little wiser (I hope!)—I can chuckle as I recall how I swelled at being pronounced the favorite of a girl so sought after by other men and how she kept me broke—but happy! I sometimes wonder how far flattery ultimately got her. I'll bet she married well!

Keep flattery in mind. It makes a good tool if you're skilled at it and able to be judicious in whom you use it on. □

13

WHAT DO YOU DO
ABOUT THE COMPETITION?

You hang in there — by ways and by means

With the exception of breathing, I don't suppose there is anything more common in a salesman's life than calling on a desirable prospect who, it turns out, is entirely satisfied with his current suppliers and sees no reason for making any changes. We call that frustrating situation *The Competition*, with a sad shake of the head. So what can you do about it? Give up?

You're confronted with an apparently indestructible stone wall. The prospect has a source from which, for a long time, he has been buying great quantities of the products you are dying to sell him. They are of excellent quality, fully equal to yours. Pricing is on the same order. Your delivery and freight allowances are no better than the other fellow's. Ditto on advertising. In short: while you can sincerely claim "just as good," you honestly don't have a thing to offer that your competitor isn't already supplying. Why *should* the customer switch his business to you?

Well — it isn't hopeless. Astrologists, soothsayers and fortune cookies to the contrary and not withstanding, people *do* change their sources of supply, given fitting circumstances — we know that. It may take time. Nevertheless, a professional would keep looking for breaks in that wall. Opportunities might arise for you to create the starting cracks, ultimately to let you through. Or, Fate might do it for you.

HE BUYS FROM HIS BROTHER-IN-LAW

Sooner or later, every salesman runs into this particular situation: your prospective customer employs a buyer who is authorized to place orders at his own discretion for the kind of products you handle, the supplying vendor determined solely by this one person. Unhappily, you find this buyer confines all his purchases in your product category to one particular source who, let's say, is represented by a fraternity brother or perhaps an even closer relative, like maybe his brother-in-law. Do you throw up your hands — forget that outfit and go on to more likely prospects?

Well — we'll assume the potential business looming up is big — very much worth much extra special effort. The amount of commission in prospect is overwhelming! This could be such a fat account; you moan — if only you could get it! So, you keep in mind vicissitudes of human nature, the exigencies of life's twists and turns, the philosophy so cogently expressed as, "Who knows?" You don't stop trying to get this company's business even though, to all outward appearances, the situation appears hopeless. (Forgive me — I said the dirty word, "hopeless" — but only for clarity in this case. That devastating word should really be crossed out of the salesman's lexicon). Reminds me of an old, whimsical tale of optimism, timeless in its application of a moral to our problem:

> *Once upon a time, there lived a cruel, heartless king bitterly regarded as a rotten s.o.b. by the people of the land. His henchmen inflicted back-breaking taxes on the population, exacted dire penalties for minor infractions of their willful rulings and eccentric laws, and altogether made life all but intolerable for his subjects.*
>
> *Consequently, the land was rife with the activities of a revolutionary underground movement. Unfortunately for the cause, calamity struck one unhappy day with the unexpected capture of the revolution's heretofore elusive leader. Dragged*

before the king in chains, the prisoner was summarily ordered to be executed within 24 hours. The wily rebel leader's mind raced, searching frantically for some idea that would help him escape the ordained fate. His eyes became fixed on the king's famous pet.

In contrast to the tyrant's cruel dealings with people, the despot was known to have a queer, soft spot in his heart for animals. In fact, he had one special, pampered pet in the form of a rare species baboon. The adored animal lay at his master's feet or sat on his lap all through the day and slept at his bedside at night. People whispered snickering remarks behind their hands about the relationship.

As the revolutionist was being waved away, the baboon left the king's lap to curiously approach the stranger. He sniffed and nuzzled the prisoner's feet, his actions accompanied with a stream of simian chatter.

"How's that again?" questioned the condemned man, seemingly asking the animal to repeat. The baboon continued his jabbering, while the prisoner paid close attention, nodding his head thoughtfully. The king gaped, taken in by this curious scene.

"Did my darling tell you you're getting what you deserve, varlet?" guffawed the ruler, and all near the royal throne roared with thigh-slapping laughter at the king's great joke.

"I didn't quite understand him," was the frowning, unexpected response. "He must have been raised in some other country or by a tribe strange to me. Somewhat different dialect — the accent throws me — "

"What the hell!" exploded the king. "Tribe? You trying to tell me you understand monkey language?"

"That depends, sire," replied the prisoner meekly. "If I may explain, your majesty?"

"Go ahead — but it better be good!"

"I was a foundling in the jungle — like Tarzan, you know? I was raised by monkeys. I learned what they were saying and could carry on a regular conversation with them. But when I was about fifteen, a group of explorers found me. They took me back to civilization and educated me."

The king scowled, but it was evident his interest had been aroused. "Tell me, you bastard — and be careful how you answer me. Is it possible that my beloved pet here could learn our language so that I might converse with him? Tell the truth now, or you'll be tortured unmercifully until you pray for death!"

The prisoner fell abjectly to his knees. "O your majesty sir — it can be done. It will take a full year but, if you will give me fifteen minutes a day and promise to release me if I am successful — which I guarantee I will be — I will teach your beloved pet to speak in the language of the land."

The king sat back, deep in thought, intrigued by this wonderful possibility. Wow — just imagine how great that would be! He looked down at his furry friend, visualizing exchanges of confidences, of philosophies, of gossiping about the people of his court. After all — what the hell — the traitor would still be in custody — suppose the scoundrel failed in his efforts — it was only for a year — he could still be executed then.

The postponement was granted. By royal decree, the prisoner was allotted fifteen minutes a day for the purpose of giving the monkey lessons in human speech.

About a week later, one of the revolutionary's lieutenants managed to get in to see their leader by dressing as a woman, pretending to be the prisoner's sister bringing him a special home-baked cake — half of which was appropriated by the guard who admitted him.

"O beloved leader," he cried, his eyes filled with tears. "What unspeakable, monstrous torture you must have suffered to extract a promise from you to teach the king's stinking monkey to speak!" He wrung his hands. "Did the pain make you bereft of your senses?"

The prisoner studied the backs of his hands. He examined

his finger nails. Finally, he replied, "I have a full year in which to make my promise good. In that length of time, you and our forces may be able to overthrow the king and set me free. Or, the animal may sicken and die, and I would persuade the stupe it was his fault for ordering such undue strain on the baboon's mind and that therefore his penance should be to set me free. Or, the king himself may take sick and die, making it possible to overwhelm his gang and our cause would be victorious.

"Or — " he hesitated. Then, with a shrugging gesture, he added, "Who knows? In a year's time — maybe the goddam monkey will speak!"

Getting back to that kingly customer who has much largesse to dispense, except that his henchman deals only with a supplier who happens to be represented by his brother-in-law: nevertheless, you are advised to hang in there! Keep in mind some of the innumerable possibilities.:

Perhaps your rival rep, sure of the business, grows fat on the job. Relaxed, complacent because he has this one big account presumably locked up, he goes out playing golf when he should be working. His lack of progress, not bringing in additional business, perhaps makes his principal unhappy, and with ill feeling developing, might lead to his termination — in which case, assuming you had kept in touch, you would be on something like even terms with his replacement, probably in a more favorable position because of already being known to the buyer. Or, the buyer might be transferred to a different department or division, perhaps leave the company to take a position elsewhere. Again, your chances are good for getting the business because you've been hanging around there — so to speak — and you start on at least even terms with the new buyer.

What is *misfortune* for one — say a broken leg — is *fortune* for another — in this example, the doctor. That ill wind of old. . . . It is possible that because of being weakened by a drastic strike, a disastrous fire, large credit losses, a major embezzlement by a trusted officer, or some other tragic circumstances, your competition might be forced out of business. Thus Fate would have provided you with that break in the stone wall. You can feel sorry for the other fellow's misfortune but, in the pragmatic business world, it's no different than playing football—your sympathies as a human being needn't necessarily stop you from taking advantage of the breaks.

Another suppose: what if it turns out that this is a case of a husband who can keep peace in his family only by patronizing his wife's brother! Naturally, he won't tell you this but he just may be secretly longing for an excuse to get rid of the guy, hoping for some damaging errors, a series of defective products, costly delays in delivery or some other such things to draw the ire of his superiors, who would then force him to get rid of the unwelcome relative—thus providing the justification he's been longing for to stave off his browbeating wife. In which event, if you are still around, you'd be in a position to take the account over.

It could even be that the buyer would decide to assert his manhood regardless of consequences and kick the brother-in-law out of his office on some occasion or other. Perhaps circumstances might be sufficiently drastic to lead him to divorce, thus making him a free agent, able to place his business wherever he pleases—like, as, with you. So—you keep in touch.

HOW DO YOU HANG IN THERE?

Persistence takes many forms. We are not concerned here with the basics of making sales calls, but for an example, let's review the procedures and results in the case of one certain old pro who settled down for a long, drawn-out campaign on the doorsteps of a highly desired account:

Chuck R. had been getting occasional small orders on one

of his lesser lines from this target prospect—barely producing enough commission to cover the applicable paper work. But, they helped him keep in touch, to foster relationship with the key buyer, to justify extra-curricular effort in behalf of a line of products which the customer was buying in huge quantities from Chuck's main competitor. He drooled at the mouth, envisioning the tremendous amounts of commission involved.

It was a classic situation: for a number of years this customer had used one particular brand. It dated back to the manufacturer's catalog number long specified on all of the company's prints. The buyer, one Walter B, was a man who knew his job. He had also been buying at times from another satisfactory supplier, one producing the same kind of components, in order to maintain a second source should something happen making it impossible for the first one to deliver. Though his liking for Chuck grew into a pleasant friendship, and he freely admitted Chuck's line was entirely equivalent, in all good conscience he could find no justification for making the necessary in-house changes that would be involved, perhaps to lose quantity price breaks in the bargain, simply to ring still another vendor into the picture.

Chuck dug in for a prolonged seige. When discussion of some matter relating to one of the insignificant orders he was getting arose, he would use it to lead into making a luncheon date with Walter, timing himself to appear at the buyer's desk a little early, thus giving him a chance to "preach the gospel" a bit. He might make some off-hand remark about his factory's revision of an item which had made such a big hit with the trade. Even though Walt failed to express much interest, at least the factory's name would be before him once again. Drops of water . . .

Chuck had learned Walt, like himself, was an enthusiastic baseball fan. When the headlines on some event ran big—the trade of an important player, a world series playoff and such, he would give Walt a ring, ask him what he thought about the situation, pretending he had called to twit Walt's judgment in such matters and for the purpose of making a small joking bet on the outcome.

Again, he would appear at Walt's desk with an oldie like, "Just happened to be in the neighborhood — you ready to do business with a *good* supplier for a change?" — which would lead inevitably to Walt asking what *he* would know about good suppliers — the kind of badinage that friends kick back and forth. If his factory had an announcement for the trade, perhaps a price change or a new catalog, Chuck would seize the opportunity for another contact by hand-delivering the item. When a new sample arrived, he would follow the same procedure to demonstrate it.

For a trade show coming up, Chuck made a point of delivering the admission tickets in person. At that time he would extract a promise from Walt to stop at his principal's booth — "just to be sociable." If *any* of his principals had a gimmick to hand out — if the giveaway had the appearance of some value — Chuck would make a point of hand delivering it in person rather than sending it, always seeking means for being kept in mind by the buyer.

These contacts were spaced far apart in order not to make the buyer tired of him. The campaign stretched over years. It took a world of patience to continue hoping. But — one day, came the break he had so long sought! Walt's company had a big and very important military contract — with deadlines, severe penalties in prospect for non-performance — a most critical deal. And in that pregnant period, by one of those inexplicable fateful coincidences, *both* of Walt's long dependable suppliers failed him at the same time!

In relating the circumstances to Chuck afterwards, Walt admitted that of late he had been putting up with a series of somewhat disagreeable happenings with the first vendor simply out of loyalty to people who had been satisfactory to deal with for many years — invoice errors, shortages in shipments and such. He was a reasonable man — "these things happen in the best of families." But the final straw in the case of that vendor was the inclusion of several defective units in a shipment of items critically needed for that all-important military contract.

It so happened that the supplier's sales manager was vacationing abroad and a young assistant took the matter in hand. Overzealous in protecting his employer's interests, instead of being concerned about the spot on which they had put the customer, he leisurely wasted precious time by officiously writing a letter, preemptorily calling for return of the questionable items for his people's inspection and decision. If the items proved really defective, credit would be issued in due course "less the usual 25% charge in such cases." He seemed to have no cognizance of the delay's consequences to the customer. (He was later fired, but by that time the account was lost anyway.)

In the other case Walt, thinking to play safe by working with his two suppliers, had also ordered a series of the critically needed components from the secondary source maintained for just such possible emergencies. But as a result of a bad traffic accident to the carrying truck, the shipment was damaged in transit, the precious parts needed destroyed beyond use. The supplier's Traffic Manager, evidently an obtuse individual, stood on his employer's legal rights, to the effect that once a shipment has been turned over to a public carrier, that shipper's responsibility ceases and from there on out, the matter has to be settled between the carrier and the consignee. He was probably right on the technical legalities but, unperturbed by the customer's frantic calls for replacements, he was not disposed to act pending adjudication of the claims that would absolve the shipper from responsibility.

On top of that, the first supplier's local salesman, depending evidently on the long-standing relationship, simply shrugged the situation off by declaring the matter was entirely in the factory's hands, that he was just a hired hand and only human, by gad — that this was factory policy and what could he do about it?

Chuck learned all those details afterwards. He only knew at the beginning of that all-but-hysterical call from Walt, to get on the horn and let him know by return phone how fast Chuck's people could supply his immediate requirements — price no object. He specified the quantities, the sizes and models, all of which with the sole minor exception of finish, were in the standard line of Chuck's principal. The excited rep called the factory, turned on the pressure and within a few hours was able to call Walt back with the good news that the shipment was already on its way to the airport, that he would have the required parts by the next day.

"Now give me your order number to cover!" Walt was delighted to confirm Chuck's bold initiative by following through with the formal order, inviting Chuck to have lunch with him that day — on him. . . .

Well, that got Chuck the account — with commissions running from two to three thousand per month, to repay him many times over for his persistence. The achievement was not the result of any great mental feat or skill or whatever. He was simply persistent enough and aware of human nature's always potential failings to "hang in there."   □

14

SMALL LINES, BIG LINES

And who's to be the Big Honcho around here?

I was eating a hot dog at one of those ubiquitous, quickie eating counters set up around convention halls, when a friend from my area came by. He ordered a sandwich. As he bit into it, he grimaced. Characteristic of such Shows, we made the usual criticism of the food situation. "Ever wonder what became of blotting paper?" he asked. "I can tell you. They use it to make sandwiches for these conventions." We exchanged the usual "How's things?", answered with the usual, "I'm doing a lot of business — sure busy — but I don't know if I'm making any money or not." That usual cliche over with, he whispered confidentially that the real excitement was his prospects of being appointed to represent a certain very big line. He held up two crossed fingers, symbolizing his hope.

"You're out of my class," I commented.

He looked at me narrowly and made a grinning observation. "I don't know the details of your business, of course, but the way I size you up is that you do a small but wery, wery profitable business. You're making money!"

"I admire your perspicacity," and I bowed. About that time, a passing friend hailed him and he excused himself to catch up with the other.

That was about ten years ago. I heard later that he got his big line all right. Really a big one. He's still in business today, too — going big, making lots of money, I presume.

Me? I'm retired. Quite comfortable, thank you.

That true littl anecdote is offered only to illustrate opposing principles, with every man having to decide for himself which he is going to follow. To have a big or small rep business is not always of one's own volition, although if you happen to be a very strong-minded, self-believing individual, determined to be in charge of your own life, you may be cast in the role of a small but — hopefully! — prosperous rep. On the other hand, by your own searching out, luck, fate or whatever, you may latch on to what my friend would call a "wery, wery big line," followed by finding yourself operating a huge, multiperson organization — with its continuance largely dependent on the "big" line.

In comparing the two situations, is there something derogatory to be said about the rep who prefers to stay clear of very big lines? That he's afraid to tackle a big operation? His competence too doubtful to be entrusted with a big line? Too lazy to undertake the heavy job of handling big lines? Can't get them anyway — sour grapes?

The answer to all those suppositions is, I don't think so. Not necessarily. Some have a reason in their own minds which justifies deliberately holding the size of the business to what they consider adequate proportions, only big enough to serve their ends. That reason is — very simply, in a word — independence. As the July Fourth political speeches like to put it — and it is so true — if you want to preserve your liberty, you have to pay for it.

A man who has the courage, the self-confidence needed to give up a good position, with its dependable regular paychecks, all the fringe benefits and a career pretty well mapped out for him, to exchange that sinecure for the risks, the hard work, the long hours, the trials and tribulations of being in business for himself, has made his decision motivated in the main by exactly that last phrase — to be his own boss. When he chose the difficulties of manufacturers' representation for an occupation, he was seeking not only economic goals but to be master of his own fate, in charge of his own person.

> *The sales manager of one of the country's well-known corporations was giving a talk at one of our association meetings. "I'm aware that it is unusual for a company like us to use reps rather than direct factory salesmen, but we prefer reps. We understand them." Fine! Sounded good! "Whenever we put on a new rep, we have him and his key men at the plant for a week, during which they get an indoctrination in our policies." Indoctrination? Achtung? Somehow the word brought up visions of Communists, of the soap-box orator shaking an accusing finger in the face of his listeners, "You don't like crim with strawmberries? Comes the revolution you'll eat crim with strawmberries and you'll like it!"*
>
> *"Indoctrination"? Well—not unreasonable, but—*
>
> *"We have a corporate course of instructions," he continued, "which the rep is to study. It sets out determination of functions in the various situations we meet. From this, he is instructed in the makeup of the departments with which he will deal, whom to contact, names of the department heads who make whatever decisions may be required...."*
>
> *Like a military manual for G.I.'s? Responsibility without authority? Decisions by department heads? What's different from being an out-and-out employee of this company other than that you get no regular paycheck or any fringe benefits with the job?*
>
> *On the other hand, it pays like a "big line" should!*

In short: to be a direct factory employee with the comforts of a dependable income and all the other advantages that go with a job nowadays—or—

To be a professional sales representative, serving a number of manufacturers' interests—a small businessman, proceeding on his own competence, under his own volition, free of what he may consider unpleasant working conditions—in short, independence . . .

It's still a free country. The choice is yours. ☐

15

THE SALESMAN SWITCH PLOY

If at first you don't succeed,
maybe somebody else will

Yours is a well established agency, employing several salesmen. One of these associates — let's call him Joe — a crack man, one of your best performers, has tried everything he knows to get the account of a certain highly desired customer, without success. He can't explain why. It's puzzling. You feel the products offered have decided quality or price advantages for the referenced company — yet, for reasons not apparent, somehow Joe can't crack the account. So what do you do? Well, as a professional, at least you're going to give it the salesman switch try before conceding defeat.

Joe has been ushered out of the picture. Last time he called on the prospect, he politely said thanks for the consideration etc., etc. Maybe that isn't necessary — anyway, he stops calling. In his place you've decided to try another man — whose handle is Bill. Let's say, that is you. In all probability, Joe will try to prepare you with an outpouring of information about the prospect. He's only human. He's chagrined, perhaps feels he's lost face. He'll try to be sincere, but it's best to disregard what he tells you other than bare essentials, like names and positions. If he actually did know why he failed, he would have taken steps to correct it. No — it's best for you to come in fresh, with no preconceived prejudices. Just pick up the pieces and go to work.

One day, you drop in on the company's target buyer. You tell him some changes have been made, that Joe has been shifted to another territory, that it is you who will be calling on him hereafter. Anticipate the likelihood of a quick dismissal; for instance, you bring a new catalog to present to him — literature is always acceptable. Doe he have a copy? Is he familiar with all the products described? How about the new ones? Perhaps you've just received new price sheets and you thought he might want a copy for his files; at the same time, you sort of offhandedly ask how your new prices compare to those he has been paying. *Your aim is to get started talking* about your cause with him.

And how is business? Might not the use of our items (name one or two) improve your profit structure, Mr. Buyer — enhance the appearance of your device — or do a better job for you because of such great features? (For better or worse — he is mentally comparing you to Joe, you know.) Encourage him to talk.

Let's say, more or less perfunctorily but sooner or later, he probably tells you your products have been considered and they have been rejected. To which you absently nod — you've heard him — but you're somewhat puzzled. You don't quite get the message. Since this item (name it) is being used in such huge quantities — you wonder if *this* such-and-such a point was brought to his attention before — so many people do overlook it — and you bring to his attention some obscure feature of what you're selling, explaining its purpose. You're shaking his negative determination a bit.

If that doesn't get you going into further discussion of your products and he is positive in his negative stance, indicating that he wants you to leave, you gracefully acquiesce. But — as you near the exit — before you go — (something like the "just-happened-to-remember" shtick of that "Colombo" TV detective) — you are reminded that you have to make a report to your office (or to your principal) on the outcome of this call. Would he mind answering just one or two quick questions?

One or two queries would be — and you make a big show of writing this out — the reasons for his rejection. After perhaps another minor question, you shake your head, politely expressing doubt that he is right in the reasons he gives for the rejection. You turn back to tell him why. You get going. . . . Perhaps you will make one or two more calls on him. Finale: in time, you get your first order from the recalcitrant. . . .

Well, I'm not really trying to write a play here. You may have an entirely different approach — but to the same end. The foregoing is simply to guide you in what might be described as maneuvering a second attack so that, on the same offerings, the *second* man gets the business where the first man failed.

It's not nice to fool human nature, but it's smart to understand it. In order to be successful in turning our prospect into a customer, it sometimes becomes necessary to take devious or circuitous routes. It so happens that whether a buyer acts like a man-eating tiger or a pussycat, in actual fact the guy is nevertheless human (even though you may question the fact about some buyers you know!).

If you'll grant that, you'll realize he will have prejudices. These characteristics of human nature create profit or zilch for us, as the case might be — but whether deep-seated, hidden or superficial, justified or irrational, let us consider generally what the most likely prejudices may be as applied to salesmen. For instance:

Joe may be a bit on the aggressive side — perhaps sometimes over-enthusiastic about a product, — too much so for this particular buyer's liking . . . Joe may be quite verbose. A faraway expression appears in his eyes that indicates he isn't following what the buyer is saying — which is bad for the latter's ego and affects his desire to write Joe orders. That is, Joe may be something of a non-stop talker who doesn't go into the pits long enough for the buyer to say what he thinks may be the product's drawbacks or to explain what his own preferable requirements may be. . . . Joe may smell of dead cigarette or pipe smoke, a characteristic of the smoker's clothes or perhaps exhudes too strongly the scent of an after-shave lotion, turning the buyer off from keeping his attention on the product being discussed. . . .

Joe may have happened to drop a thoughtless, off-hand but unwelcome political opinion or, particularly bad, he might have made some presumably light remark of a religious nature—not necessarily extreme one way or another, but possibly displeasing to the buyer, who is perhaps a man of profound religious convictions. . . . Still worse, Joe may have told an ethnic joke—one he thought harmless, but funny—except that, as often happens in this country, the buyer was a third generation American descendant, an unrecognized member of the people being derided. . . .

Joe may have been a careless dresser—pants need pressing, shoes need shining, wears a crumpled shirt reminiscent of the "ring-around-the-collar" TV commercial. Or, he might be given to wearing sport shirts, without a tie—which, unreasonable though that might be, somehow gets identified unfavorably in this particular buyer's mind with the product, causing his disrespect for Joe's attire to depreciate the product. Some may heartily disagree, citing the modern trend toward comfort in clothing as well as style. Unfortunately, many a man has been swept away by the unseen rip tides of human nature—and to be unreasonable *is* a characteristic of some people.

So many things more are possible to have prejudiced this buyer against him. Joe may be one who disregards formal buying hours or the need for making appointments and has a way of barging in unannounced, causing the buyer to think of him as damned presumptuous. . . . Joe uses profanity freely, not realizing that this particular prospect retains the habits of boyhood training and dislikes hearing the Lord's name being taken in vain. . . .

Perhaps Joe unconsciously crowds too close to the prospect, who shies away from physical intimacy — at least with a man — similar to Joe's habit of vigorously grasping and shaking a man's hand whenever he meets him, disregarding the fact that there are those who dislike the sweaty palm greeting — especially knowing that the great show of love and affection is only part of a salesman's pitch. . . .

Or, Joe may have a habit, unthinking perhaps, of reading papers lying before him on the buyer's desk, which the prospect finds annoying . . . or —

Of course, if our composite "Joe" were actually afflicted with all the possible drawbacks just enumerated, unquestionably he would have been a miserable failure and out of selling long ago. But, as indicated before, Joe *is* good at his job, so what is the answer? Why didn't he get the business in question, while Bill did? Simply this: that a man may be at fault *in only one respect* yet **that** could be the one to kill him with this buyer to whom we've been referring!

Joe might have been a fine, shining model of what makes a good salesman, completely free of those faults we spoke of *except* let's say, he is a bit careless about keeping his fingernails clean. This buyer might have been the offspring of an old fashioned home of the kind where cleanliness is important enough to be all but a fetish. Which might have him fastidiously exaggerating this minor untidiness into considering Joe something of a slob — in turn, closing his mind to Joe's sales talk. The irony of this: a second salesman might, conceivably, have some or many of the distracting faults we listed — all by-passed by the buyer, the only thing turning him off being just some one particular characteristic which he finds offensive.

I can't leave this subject without a word or two about one of the oddest manifestations of human nature one sometimes encounters. That is a dislike for profanity by some people who are themselves the very ones habitually using it. I don't know why — for an explanation of why the other fellow's use of such expletives annoys them, you'll have to consult your favorite psychologist—I only know it as one more bit of curiosa in human nature.

That brings to mind the incident one time when I had succeeded in establishing one of my lines with a distributor in replacement of a line he had previously stocked. Holding forth on what he expected of my line and why he had dropped that of my competitor, he spoke of how much he had always disliked their sales agent.

"And another reason I couldn't stand the bastard," he said, "was his language. He always had such a goddam vulgar way of talking. Kinda embarrassing, you know?"

"Yeh," I agreed, "Embarrassing."

We're dealing with the eccentricities of human nature when we're trying to sell. Whether justified or irrational, people are subject to prejudice against their fellow men. Which is why the salesman switch ploy is an important method to keep in your firm's bag of tricks.   □

16

GETTING IN TO SEE THE BUYER

Know your human nature

Every rep has his "the-world-is-down-on-me" moments, especially acute when he feels a particular so-and-so whose job it is to do the buying for a certain important prospect, just hates salesmen. Which, of course, isn't so—at least, not always!

Employ empathy. Put yourself in his place. Think of how it is when you yourself are the object of someone trying to sell you things; compare to that buyer getting pounded away at all day long. How do you react? But, you say, he gets *paid* to deal with the vendors. Well, yes,—you've got a point there.

Which brings up *this* point: whatever may be the circumstances in individual cases—don't ever lose sight of the absolute but often forgotten fact that BUYERS *need* SELLERS. *He needs you* (and reasonable facsimiles!) as well as you need him He *must* purchase things for his company in order that it continue to exist—and for him to retain his job! Those "things" may very well be products such as you have to sell. Regardless of the means necessary to place those "things" before him, if you sincerely believe you are offering a product that will work more efficiently for his company, function faster for them, save labor or money—in other words, a *better* "thing," or if your target is a merchant who can resell your products and thereby make money for himself, that buyer is not necessarily doing *you* a favor by granting you the time necessary to consider what you have to offer. It may very well be the other way around!

Of course, it is using your time to best advantage and augers well for the success of your call if you have a definite appointment, with the prospect setting aside time for you. If you can manage that, great, but—suppose the buyer has regular "buying hours" and he expects you as well as others like you to call on him during the specifically authorized periods—why phone for an appointment? Because—it's thinking in terms of our old friend human nature again. You're employing a bit of psychology that has you standing out from the crowd. By inference, you impress him with the fact that *your* time is valuable.

He has salesmen assaulting his ear drums hour after hour—his mind sometimes goes a little numb with it all. But when you phone beforehand, *asking* if he will be available at the specific time you offer, the inference is that you have something particularly meaningful for him and want to make sure he will have the time—otherwise, you tell him, you will be glad to come by at some other hour or day—at his convenience—because you really *do* want him to see this "new" thing when he can give it the attention it deserves. You're going out of town and have this new sample to show him, a new catalog, a new price list, or whatever you can come up with as a reason for *mutually* agreeing on the time for you to call

With *that* accomplished, upon your arrival you can truthfully tell his receptionist you have an appointment and you sail right in. Likewise, since he is expecting you, you are pretty well assured that you are going to get his good attention! Of course, you have to have that *something* "new" or in some way different prepared by way of justifying his special attention. He might even give you a time outside of his "buying hours," when that reception room full of salesmen wanting to get at him won't be there.

It's the little touches, the fine points, some commonly used but others frequently overlooked, that make the professional. For example: hand your calling card to the receptionist and ask for the man you want to see while, at the same time, pronounce your name — *distinctly*. Don't just rattle it out (a) be articulate so that she will transmit it correctly to your target and (b) even if it's a common name, to help her memorize it, to tie it in with you in particular, to encourage being greeted as a friend the next time you arrive.

Cultivate those receptionists! They can be most helpful. There was this rep who made a practice of bringing a flower (just one — not a bunch!) for the receptionist every time he called, usually accompanied with some pseudo-romantic speech. That little gesture was sure to make her a bosom friend — uh — sorry — just meant a good friend. Very often, though others had been waiting to see the buyer, he would be ushered right in soon as he showed.

By cultivating the friendship of the receptionists, and also the secretaries, and any assistants to your various Mr. Bigs (buyers), I mean that you make every effort to engage them in converstion whenever possible, *keeping the subjects on Mr. Big* — trying to learn from them whatever you possibly can about the kind of man he is. Does he like sports — an excellent and usually popular subject; one which, later, when you call on Mr. Big, gives you an opener for the start of conversation with him. Ask them: Did he attend the recent trade show? Opinions of it? Has he had or is he going on a vacation, and where? Is he a golfer, a fisherman; other enthusiasms? Dig for any bits of information about Mr. Big which you can bring into your later discussions, to make use of in furthering your friendship with him.

If you are a smoker, take your last puff before you come into your prospect's presence. If you have to wait in the reception lobby, refrain from smoking — chew gum or something if you must. Keep in mind today's antagonism to cigarettes. If a non-smoker, your man may look upon you with pity for your enslavement to the weed, with distaste for your presence because he is allergic to second-hand smoke. He may be one who recently quit himself, and won't be happy with another smoking in his presence, thus putting a strain on his will power. Better yet—if at all within your power—refrain from smoking anywhere near the time preceding the call, keeping in mind that a smoker's clothes smell of stale smoke—particularly noticeable to the non-smoker and very likely offensive. Time enough to light up after leaving.

"Mr. Buyer isn't seeing salesmen today." Suppose you're making your first call on Mr. Big. The receptionist eyes your briefcase, sizes you up and notifies you shortly that Mr. Big doesn't see salesmen on Friday or after 3 p.m. or whatever happens to be that particular house rule about salesmen calling that you seem to be violating.

Let me personalize this because I went through it in my business life again and again. I can testify, it works. I was always conscious of the fact that I just couldn't afford to confine my calling time to the various eccentric, nonmatching mixture of periods that buyers set up as "buying hours." Not only would I be killing off too much of my working day, but I didn't relish contending with my fellow reps in there, fighting for the buyer's time and attention. And also, I might as well admit, my ego would become involved. I just didn't particularly care to have some two-bit, gum-chewing little blondie telephone operator stopping *me* from doing my job. My favorite approach to the problem then was an act that would go something like this:

Upon hearing the young lady's dictum, I ostentatiously squint at my watch. Then, with eyes narrowed, looking fixedly off into space, I mutter (but distinctly enough for her to hear) "I've just got to make that plane," as though to myself. Then to her, "I have some information from my factory for Mr. B. but I won't be able to give it to him without making a special call out here again—and that, I'm afraid, won't possibly be for some time." Shrug of my shoulders. "Well— here's my card—extend my apologies to your boss—you can tell him I tried—it's not my fault," and, slowly turning toward the door, "If it's important, tell him to write or phone me."

It's a pretty good possibility that, her concern aroused, she will call after you, "Well, just a moment, sir." You stare down at your watch again, with a worried expression. (Easy—a deep frown, a bit of head-shaking—that's all you need!) The girl, now quite impressed with these histrionics, phones in to Mr. B., telling him there's a gentleman here who "made a special trip to see you with some important information for you. He has to catch a plane so he won't be able to get back again." She listens a moment, reads your name to him from your card and turns to me with a "Mr. B. will see you now."

Go back and read the script again—note the key words and actions for this little scenario—the watch bit, the vague observation about catching a plane (could be reference to another critical appointment you can't miss) the repeating of "again," the reference to having "information for Mr. B.," the inference of it being important to him, the speaking of "my factory," common enough among reps but giving her the impression that you are really a bit shot *owner* of a factory—these things, re-phrasing them in *her* words given urgency as *she* will do it, gets you in.

Of course, you've got to be supplied with justification for your act after you're seated in Mr. B.'s office. It shouldn't bee too difficult. Perhaps it can be a bingo card that he filled out and sent to your principal—you're here to give him the data *he* called for. It might be a significant price reduction soon to be in effect and you're there to warn him so that he can take advantage of the information, or a new version of an interesting product you honestly feel has reason to be of value to him. Perhaps he left a request at a trade show for a catalog or other information which you are taking the time to personally deliver. It's up to you to be prepared with some fairly plausible excuse for the act you are putting on to gain entrance to his innter sanctorum.

Keep it in mind. I can tell you that, while not always, when it was necessary I frequently found this little act a successful ploy.

A sure-fire followup practice that will make you most welcome next time you call, by way of creating and retaining a customer's good will, is letting him know in a specific way that his interests are on your mind. Suppose you have been given an order of considerable size on which, without anyone necessarily speaking of it, he must be aware you will make a substantial commission. A day or so after processing the order, you might drop him a note (do this in your own handwriting) — much more impressive than a conventional verbal "thank you," telling him that you've sent the order on its way, that you are personally going to follow it through to make sure it will be handled to his complete satisfaction — a kind of informal version of the order acknowledgment which he will receive from your principal but which you have thus prestamped with *your* personality, helping to build his confidence in the fact that he can deal with *you*, right here, on his own home grounds.

For ordinary, fair-size orders, even though they aren't going to make you rich, it's good practice to send a personal letter of thanks to the buyer, assuring him that his business will receive your good service, etc. This can follow the wording of a form letter which your secretary can automatically type out, ready for you to sign at the proper time.

These little touches — it doesn't take too awful much — but how they can count! As the prestigious Wall Street Journal once put it, one ten-thousandth of an inch makes the difference between a smooth shave and blood.   □

17

IS THE BUYER YOUR REAL TARGET?

In-depth selling

You are a perceptive man, always on the ball, never over-looking possibilities for adding new customers to your list. You have reason to believe — by bingo card, by your knowledge of the kind of trade existing in your territory, by one of their ads perhaps — but, regardless of how you find out, you become aware that the ZYX Corporation is one you should be calling on. So, you do — to learn they manufacture a device or a series of products, perhaps a machine of some sort — anyhow, whatever it is they make, you have a most fitting component they could use. Not only that, but if you could get them to adopt this little jewel into their production, the resulting orders would loom up very big on your commission statements which would naturally follow. You'd like that.

Unfortunately, you find the buyer to whom you are directed is one of those who knows little and probably cares less about what goes on in the engineering department of his company. He's perfectly willing to talk with you but, despite the superiorities of your offering, he is one of those pencil pushers who wouldn't make a move to replace the brand already in presumably satisfactory use, he having heard no complaints about it. He's got enough problems, he tells you plaintively, without going out of his way to stir up a quiescent situation. He hopes you will be sympathetic, understanding, and thanks for the nice lunch.

This is a tough one, indeed. What do you do?

Situations of this kind are all too common and should be anticipated with a strategy which might be described as the Determination of Who's Who in that company. With due allowance for differences in one industry from another, if at all sizable, you can expect to encounter what amounts to a Chain of Procurement. The links are known by various titles or descriptive terms peculiar to a given business of which, in a general way, the following are facsimiles, with each having various degrees of influence in the determination of which products the company buys.

1. *Manager or Director of Procurement.* He may be an executive in the person of the president, the owner, or one of the company's employees high in management. The *least* he does is to direct buying policies, amounts to be expended over a given time, and when.

2. *Quality Control.* The term, or its equivalent, indicates exactly what this department does. At various stages, perhaps at the very beginning or while in production, that which the company buys comes under the scrutiny of those in this department and must conform to the standards they set. They can make or break productive results for you.

3. *Design Engineers.* Probably in one way or another having the most influence on how far you get with this company, though that fact may not be readily apparent. Chances are that what your prospective customer makes starts here, to include specification of its components. Some one "designer" or a group of such experts create an item, maybe a series of articles, machines or equipment of some kind — whatever it is for which this company is in business to make and sell.

It is possible that the company exists because someone once invented, contrived, devised or developed something for which a market existed or was developed, which led to starting this company. It may be a very big company by the time you arrive on the scene and try to get into their picture, and also, they may have one or more engineers continually occupied with making available more new products for your prospective customer to manufacture.

If your component is quite different from the one the company has been using—perhaps in size, in mounting or other configuration—it's a pretty good guess that if your offering were to be considered favorably, it would be turned over to this department for studying changes or modifications necessary in order to use it in the designated application.

4. *The buyer.* Wondering when we'd get around to this paper jockey, eh? Well, okay—he or she, of course, is the one who actually issues the orders you are so anxious to get into your hot little hands—the person with whom you ordinarily would deal, for better or worse. If this is a sizable company and you don't get past this buyer's desk, your chances are pretty slim for getting the big order. It's not just a matter of the inertia or apathy on this employee's part that we spoke about previously. It's because by the time it becomes necessary for the order to be written out, specific requirements are already way down stream. The color, the model, the material of which it is made, the quantity—all the main provisions governing the referenced component requirement may be presumed to have been pretty well determined before it gets to the buyer in the form of a requisition. Even if the referenced component isn't spelled out by brand name, to land the order at this late date becomes a forlorn grab-bag deal.

From which you may gather, the rep who digs the deepest into making acquaintance with the *personnel* of that prospective customer, is the one most likely to get his principal's name on that order. So—how do you do that?

Well, first: you ask! Question anyone who might be presumed to know who your basic target is—in this instance, say, the one or more persons designated as design engineers. Perhaps the girl at the reception desk can tell you or you might work the information out of one of the company's buyers. In some cases, something might arise that would have you being led through the plant. Keeping your eyes open, you might spot some young fellow in shirt sleeves, humped over a drawing board, the very lad likely to be your real target. If the company should happen to have a cafeteria into which outsiders are sometimes invited, perhaps you can get the buyer to let you buy him lunch there—where, as you accompany him, he will hail fellow employees to whom in turn he will introduce you, among them possibly being the very man you want to know. Or— ask to meet him!

Suppose you put out a particularly attractive "giveaway"— a calendar, a crossover chart of American measurements to the metric system, a nice pen. Etc. Tell the receptionist (after giving her one, of course) or the buyer, that you would like to present one to each "key" person in that organization—and could you have *their* names and positions? The receptionist is probably your best bet—she wouldn't be bothered wondering if you had an ulterior motive—and she is very apt to have a complete roster at hand of the company's personnel, from which you might manage somehow to excerpt the names and positions of your targets. She could be the talkative kind, maybe wants to be impressive—who makes a big thing of telling you so-and-so is worth cultivating. (Note, I repeat—how desirable it is to make a friend of that receptionist—she can be helpful in so many ways).

Perhaps your prospect manufacturing customer issues drawings having to do with their products. Such drawings might show the name of the draftsman/engineer, who could happen to be the man you want to know.

Well, inasmuch as such situations vary all over the map, it

is difficult in a discussion like this to single out just who the decision makers may be in a given company other than the so-called "buyer," but it is hoped the foregoing may serve as guidelines leading into *your* way of searching them out. You have to dig. Did anybody tell you being a rep was going to be easy? ☐

18

BUSINESS IS WHERE YOU FIND IT

—but you never know from where until you look

It is our American habit at times of by-passing the inexhaustible richness of expression available in usage of the English language by curious transpositions of words or phrases. Taken literally, the locutions sometimes convey meanings just the opposite or radically different from their correct pedantic definitions. An example would be, "You never know where you are going to get business."

A foreigner, having learned academic English in his own country, might be justified in thinking that declaration was deprecatory salesmanship, that the speaker literally was confessing he didn't know his job. Whereas, of course, it's simply an old expression to the effect that business can be found in unexpected places. In which connection, you might consider a few possibilities perhaps outside of your usual port o'calls.

Daily newspapers carry legal notices of "intent to engage in business," of fictitious business names filed, of building permits for new construction and so on. Usually the announcements mean establishment of new places of business. Such enterprises might use something you sell. People starting new ventures expect to be needing new things and are in a buying mood. Equipment for their offices? Tools? Air conditioning? Calculators? Computer terminals? Whatever! If they seem to be possible prospects in your line, let them know you're in business by mail, phone or, where warranted, by personal call, with a view to selling in your own or a principal's name, as conditions may govern. If not that directly, you may uncover business for your distributors.

         *   *   *

Are you in some branch of the building supplies industry or associated therewith? Check with City Hall periodically for names and addresses appearing on permits issued by the building departments for new construction, to be followed up by mailings or personal calls according to how you size up the prospective buyers of your products.

         *   *   *

But of far greater potential: consider your city, county and state, to say nothing of miscellaneous military supply centers and Federal government agencies, these being among the business world's very profitable customers. Look up their buying offices in your phone book, check the procurement routines and requirements of such governing bodies as related to your category of products. For such information, search out people with titles like Procurement Manager or some version thereof. (Later, I'll speak of one of the oddities of dealing with government agencies.)

         *   *   *

Check the public notices of "bids awarded" for the names and applicable details of the successful bidders. Perhaps the winners are potential prospects for your products.

List yourself or your principals (as may be required to comply with the formalities) on their bid request lists. While in the case of public bodies lowest pricing is most likely to get the award, it doesn't always follow; other factors may override price. Which (just for a moment of relaxation), brings up a story:

> *Every so often, a movement starts for digging a tunnel under the English Channel from England to France. It always fails. One year, the project actually got to the bidding stage. The official committee's chairman opened the sixth bid submitted by one "S. Colberg & Son." He fastened his monocle securely in place, frowned and looked around the table.*

*"Does anyone know this company?" All shook their heads.
The name was completely unfamiliar. Since such a project
would obviously have to be carried out by responsible people,
the chairman started to toss the bid into a wastepaper basket
but one committeeman raised a restraining hand.*

*"These bids have to be made public. There might be
trouble if we don't have justification for rejecting the lowest
bid. I move we investigate and then we can drop it."*

*It was agreed. The chairman ordered a secretary to check
the bidder's status with his bank, which was noted on the bid.
That institution reported the company was small but long
established, a respectable business enterprise. The committee
extended an invitation for Mr. Colberg to appear before
them. He turned out to be a baldheaded, friendly little
gentleman, quite willing to answer searching questions. In
reply to how many employees in his company, he answered,
"Just me and my son, Samuel."*

*"But, sir!" frowned the questioning chairman. "Just how
do you and your son propose to dig this tunnel?"*

*"I expect Samuel will start from Calais on the French coast
and me from Dover, England, and we'll dig toward each
other until we meet about the middle of the channel."*

"But suppose you miss each other?"

"Then you'll get two tunnels."

Sorry, gentle readers—I just couldn't resist such a tempt-
ing lead-in to one of my favorite stories. Getting back to business: the products used by our various governing and military outfits run the gamut in variety. As Jimmy Durante
would say, "Everybody can get into the act." Items may be
required from paper clips to computers. A friend told me
about once seeing a military request for 250 female mules.
(One may wonder what the lady libbers might have to say
about this presumably chauvinistic insistence on females as
beasts of burden.)

But that recalls a true story related to me by Bill B., an

old-time distributor friend of mine, when he was struggling to keep his small business going during World War II in the face of merchandising shortages for civilian use. Talk about strange military requirements!

>   *Bill was on the bid list of a nearby Marine Corps supply depot. Poring over a four-page listing of a mixed variety of items needed by the depot, his eyes popped as he came to an item reading, "25,000 prophylactics, rubber only." He scrutinized the specification over and over again. It was entirely clear — evidently they meant it!*
>
>   *The oddity of such a requirement took him back to his own wartime experiences — on leave in Paris — liberty — "the Mademoiselles from Armentieres" of World War I fame (and of his acquaintance) — to the items issued by the government that created the "g.i." addition to the language — but Uncle Sam hadn't thought to be that concerned about us fellows at the time, that he could remember! . . . Twenty-five thousand condoms? How soldiering has changed!*
>
>   *So Bill did some researching and found that one of the nationally known tire manufacturers produced condoms. A reply to his enquiry and a quote came back promptly, with the admonition that, with war conditions prevailing, priority rating would be required. That presented no problem for a military customer. Bill filled out the bid, sent in his quotation and received the properly qualified order. The deal wound up with a neat profit for him.*
>
>   *About a year after the war ended, he received another bid for the same item, again for 25,000 pieces. He filled out the usual bid form and got the order. This time, his curiosity could not be contained. Instead of sending the package on after receiving the shipment, he placed it in the trunk of his car and drove to the supply base. Calling for the Purchasing Officer, he was told to deliver the shipment to the receiving department in back of the building.*
>
>   *"I'll do that, sir," said Bill, "but if it isn't classified*

information — would you please tell me what in the hell the Marine Corps does with so many condoms?"

The officer chuckled. "Come along with me." He led the way through the office back door into a storage room of the huge warehouse. There the officer pointed out what seemed to be an all-but-endless row of racks filled with rifles. Taking one of the guns out of the rack, the officer showed Bill how a covering rubber, stretched to transparency, was pulled down over the length of the barrel.

"During the war, when the Marines were making a landing," he explained, "these things were used to cover the rifles, thereby helping to keep them from getting wet. Now that they are here in storage, can you think of a better or cheaper way for protecting the rifles from dust and dampness?"

*   *   *

If you are a stocking rep and function as the vendor, you will do well to pay punctilious attention to the exactitude of details in billing government agencies. I learned! by virtue of an incident that happened long ago but which I'm sure still pertains, and which wasn't at all funny. Back in the days when I was a radio distributor, I got an order from a division of the Air Corps at Wright Field in Ohio for a list comprising eleven items — none amounting to much money but, it so happened, I had them all in stock and so was able to ship promptly.

When I made out the invoice, most of the items whose unit price was extended, came out with several mils. Where the extended mils came to five or more, I rounded the cents off to the next highest amount — if less than five, I dropped the mils. The result of my grand total (gad! I can still remember the figure!) was $278.60 which, it developed much later, if calculated with mathematical precision, totaled four mils lower than if I had carried each item out to the third place.

My billing was summarily rejected as incorrect. The form

with my returned invoice gave no details. It took pages and pages and an exchange of a number of letters over a period of four months before I learned that the rejection was because my total and that of the Accounts Payable clerk differed—by a fraction of a cent!—and in the government's favor, at that! I finally learned the name of a superior officer—it was one Captain Mervin Jacobs—and when I wrote my heart-rending saga to him personally, the situation received common sense attention and I got my check.

Well—these things happen. Nothing worthwhile comes easy when you're trying to make money. But a nice thought to keep in mind: happiness is receiving a check for something you've sold to the military, to the city, the county, the state or some branch of the Federal government because it's like getting a refund on your taxes!   ☐

19

ON APPLYING FOR A LINE

How do you sell yourself?

It is something of a paradox when a *good* salesman can have difficulty carrying on a fully informative, meaningful exchange of correspondence with a prospective principal having to do with his ability to perform as a rep. One of the unfortunate anomalies sometimes encountered even among college graduates is inability to promote oneself in writing, although the difficulties diminish when the opportunity for a face-to-face meeting arises. But whether in writing or in person, following are some of the guidelines having to do with perhaps less obvious but important information that the sales manager will want to have—even if you have to tape it and send him the recording! At any rate, no matter in what form it is put:

Of course you will specify the product division of the industry in which you operate. This should be accompanied with some detail for identifying the class of trade you call on, such as whether or not distributors only or manufacturers or retailers or research laboratories and so on—that your calls are on those in the category in which you specialize, or to a mixture of all of them, as the case may be. Discuss and name some of the better known. Point up how well you do with them. If it is *you* who sold the distributor who won a big prize for winning a sales contest, mention that. It might be of special interest to categorize your lines. That is, if you are in hardware are your main lines of the fasteners, hand tools and adhesives variety or in portable power tools, aerosol products, heavy equipment? If in electronics, are you in consumer products, audio or semiconductors—and so on.

If you employ, say, two salesmen and an office girl, don't stop at saying you have three employees. Your prospective sales manager wants to be given confidence in whom he appoints, to know what *kind* of guys would be calling on *his* customers, telling people *they* represent *his* factory. Your Joe is a degree engineer, about to receive his MBA by virtue of taking night courses and that his technical background always proves so important to the customers, that Bill has been calling on the local trade for years and knows everyone on a first-name basis, that the girl who answers your phone is more than a receptionist, that she functions in part as an excellent inside salesperson because she has such aptitude with mechanical things—etc., etc. Be sure to mention if any of your people have advanced degrees including, of course, yourself. Emphasize aggressiveness in going after business, talk about know-how; stay clear of giving ages unless you particularly want to present yourself as a youthful but *experienced* firm and be prepared to back up the latter.

If you are a member of sales organizations such as MANA, ERA, or your local Chamber of Commerce, scientific or engineering societies, be sure you say so. Such affiliations and the year your business was established, are mute but pertinent testimonials to your reputation for responsibility.

Something all too often overlooked by reps is the advantage of making your bank manager a friend. Inasmuch as you may not be contemplating making loans at the bank, this may not strike you as important. But—it is! There are times when you *will* need to give reference for some purpose or another. It is always impressive when you can name *the manager* personally, as well as giving the name of your bank—especially referring to him familiarly by his first name. And, it's just possible you may go in for stocking merchandise and banks are in business for the purpose of working with you in your enterprises.

Again, there may be occasions when it can be very useful to have a *signed* letter from your friendly bank officer, stating, "to whom it may concern" that you are highly regarded, a valued client of *this* bank and have been for X number of years." (What's to be bashful? Ask! Nowadays, banks offer you gifts to come in, have coffee and let's be friends! — don't they? Full page ads?)

If you are a bit uncertain about how to get acquainted with your bank manager and if circumstances don't bring it about by themselves, force the issue. Take a straightforward approach; for instance, let's say you have just had an attractive line card printed. Tell the manager's secretary frankly that you want to meet her boss and can she arrange the proper time? At the appointed hour, bring in a copy of that line card for him. Hand it to him with the opening remark, "Just thought you might want to have this for your files on me. One of these days, I may have some special banking requirements and this will give you a good picture of what I do."

If one of your lines has a name that most people are likely to recognize, "just happen" to mention how great you've been doing in representing this manufacturer. . . Observe the officer's hands for rings: he may be a member of your lodge or wears a fraternity ring you recognize or perhaps it is a ring of unusual design — things to comment on for making conversation. Tell him how long you've been dealing with this bank and (if so) that the mortgage on your home is held by them, or speak of a loan you once made here or anything else — perhaps some unusual incident — that may show you have close relations with this bank. Don't keep him tied up more than a few minutes this first time. Break away with an honest, "Just wanted to get better acquainted Mr. ___ . Maybe we can have lunch some time?"

Now you have a nodding acquaintance with him. One day, you "just happen" to be in the bank at a quarter of noon; you get his attention and ask, "How about that luncheon? Can you make it today?" If the answer is negative, try tentatively to arrange for a nearby future date . . . And one word more: if you do have something definite in the way of banking business to take up with them, try not to let them shunt you off on some lesser employee. Head for that head man! If he turns you over to someone else, that's all right — the point has been made. You've let him know you're doing business with his bank.

When applying for that new line, send along a photocopy of the bank letter. It will have a good measure of impact. Your prospective sales manager knows a bank wouldn't write such a letter for just anybody! (P.S. Note, I say bank "*manager*". Lesser officers are more apt to be transferred around to different branches, to wind up in your losing track of your "friend".)

Of course, your prospective principal will want to know what manufacturers you already represent. A copy of your line card will answer that. A rep who doesn't *have* a line card roster will be considered as not knowing his business (right!) or that, for some reason of his own, he doesn't want prospective sales managers to know what lines he handles. Arouse *that* suspicion in the sales executive's mind and you might as well forget his line!

That brings up a special point calling for your very best judgment. It might be advisable to explain that, while your roster appears to be lengthy, as a matter of fact most of your time is expended on such-and-such products or lines, as the case might be. Whether or not to dwell on this is something to which you should give plenty of thought, envisioning the effect it may have on this prospective sales manager, to wit: If his line *does* go well with the kind which constitute your major activities, by all means stress that fact. If it doesn't, it is best to pass it up in any case — you don't need "just another line" to clutter up your works!

Somewhat similar, but more of a black-and-white situation, is describing the territory you cover — whether you get all over the area, in depth, or that you favor certain portions because of population, or a concentration of market with heavy buying power. Refer familiarly to its size, its continual growth, how the market is always expanding, how you keep on top of it—all toward impressing your prospective sales manager with the fact that you are a knowledgeable person.

Discuss the categories of the industry in which you operate as being one-step or two-step distributors, manufacturers or whatever they may be. If you call on more than one *industry*, make that known. (If you are heavy in fasteners, wouldn't you be covering electrical trade, aircraft, building supply distributors, etc. in *addition* to typical hardware distributors?)

And finally, even though this is repeated more in detail in the chapter on publicity, it must be emphasized because it is so much more meaningful than so many reps realize; have a *good* studio picture of yourself, to accompany your solicitation of the new line. The more you personalize yourself, the more of an impression you will make. And sales managers do want to know what kind of a person this is who is wanting to represent his line. A picture helps. ☐

20

SHOULD YOU FOLLOW THE LEADER?

Or, I've got to be me!

Each year at the height of the holiday season, a rep friend of mine, now long retired, used to hold an open house party for the trade—"everybody come, y' hear"—an invitation sincerely extended to competitors and their employees just as heartily as to customers. In one day of such hospitality, Nort would pour out literally gallons and gallons of liquor, at a cost of about $2,500—and note that this was back in the Truman pre-inflation years! His office was equipped with all kinds of gourmet goodies and visitors were urged to partake. Standing invitations were issued for home-bent buyers to stop by for a quickie.

I never could decide whether or not all this conviviality was an example of shrewd business instinct, the realization of how rewarding could be the many friendships born of it, the publicity that emanated from his big-hearted hospitality or (and I think more likely), that his generosity was a manifestation of love for his fellow man, particularly encompassing those who, in common with him, were earning their living in the same industry. Perhaps it was a combination of all those things.

Another of Nort's hard-to-believe but absolutely true actions was reminiscent of Cecil B. DeMille, the famous movie director, who ordered the hundreds of extras dancing in an aristocratic ballroom scene to wear silk underwear under their formal attire, reasoning that to *act* really wealthy, one must *feel* wealthy. In a somewhat similar vein, this rep bought each of his eight salesmen Cadillacs to use in making their calls, all maintenance charged to the house — the philosophy being that *the appearance and feel of prosperity were instrumental in bringing it about*. Also, overlooking no one, a station wagon was bought for the office personnel to use in case someone had to run out for a package of cigarettes or someting. . . .

Well, those are just a few highlights of an extraordinary rep operation, of which people still speak in awe. I haven't seen my friend lately. I understand he speds most of his time on the high seas, living on his quarter-of-a-million-dollar yacht, travelling around the world. As in Hollywood, where they speak of Clark Gable as the "king," there are those who look back on Nort as a kind of "king," in manufacturer's representation.

Then there was this rep who had several big lines as well as a few of average return, in a territory somewhat thinner than that of the operator previously described. He was known to be a shrewd businessman, pragmatic, as down to earth as the shoes on his feet. He drove nothing more luxurious than an inexpensive small foreign car. He not only didn't drink himself, but he studiously avoided bringing the subject up when taking a buyer to lunch — which was usually at a good but not the most expensive of restaurants.

His operation always reflected the owner's sharp sense of economy. His salesmen were required to supply their own cars. He meticulously paid them a fair allowance, but computed strictly on the mileage racked up during the car's use for business purposes. When Christmas came along, his observance of that period extended to sending greeting cards of the kind bought in department stores on which the sender's name had to be hand written. He was known to save the carbons inserted between speed-reply stationery. When he saw paper clips lying around, probably to be thrown away, he would carefully pick them up and deposit them in a suitable receptacle.

Well, while not too many people knew it, the bitter struggle he had getting started, following a depression-made Spartan bringing up, had inculcated within him right down to his bones a pin-saving sense of thrift, to permeate his entire way of life. But—he had advanced degrees which stood him in good stead for handling high technology lines, he was extremely efficient in administering the details of his business, knew his lines thoroughly, was always well informed on the happenings in his industry, was a fluent conversationalist, with the skills of a professional psychologist at playing human angles. He attracted the best of "associates" by liberal profit-sharing plans as his business grew, and he built up a big operation. He, too, retired as a very wealthy man.

Let me tell you about just one more sales agent of my acquaintance and his starting of a brand new rep career. He acquired a roster of good lines in an extraordinarily short period of time. Older reps in the same area were amazed at how fast he did it. His success came out of a deep background in various business activities, giving him a broad fund of information to draw on in soliciting lines.

His secret was simple. He avoided trying to "steal" lines from other independent reps but, instead, as a matter of policy in solicitations, he concentrated on manufacturers who were employing salaried outside salesmen, pointing up the advantages of the independent professional system. He made an exceedingly favorable impression on sales managers as a very knowledgeable man. In one case, having sold himself by such a premise, he acquired a line that resulted in his doing a twenty-five-million-dollar business on that one line alone in the second year he had it. . . . And that rep, too, became an extremely wealthy man.

I know another rep—etc., etc. One can go on interminably, describing the operations of many reps and the success they attained. But if you believe you have only to select one of these successful ones, to emulate his way of doing it and thereby yourself come to great fortune—well, sorry, it just doesn't work that way.

Manufacturers' representation as a career is a most appropriate occupation for certain individualists. And yes, absolutely, if you're smart, you'll seize on every possible opportunity to study how the other fellow did it; the only pragmatic substitute for experience is to learn by the other fellow's. One uses the essence of his methods as guidelines to indicate the right way and the wrong way—but, always, in the final analysis, if you were destined to be an independent manufacturers' sales representative, you'll do it *your* way. *However*: before making the plunge, you would do well to determine whether or not you *are* intended for this profession.

You must approach the undertaking with the understanding that the manufacturers' representative is an executive in his own right—a business administrator—a man of many parts. That when all is said and done, he's a *salesman*. And that—to be a *good* salesman calls for certain basic qualities—plus, a sense of innovation, imagination, individualism. . . .

An initial requirement, all but mandatory, is that the powerful drive of ego should be present. Not conceit—that's different—but a satisfying, compelling, inborn need to *win*, *whatever* the prize may be. True, one should emphasize the positive but, in all good common sense, one must not overlook the negative; admittedly, this may not be upbeat but, to be realistic in this instance could save much heartache: the cold fact of it is that the somewhat esoteric manufacturers' sales representation as an occupation just is not for everybody. Not by a long ways.

If I may be forgiven that old cliché—this is where the "round peg in the square hole" applies. You could be extremely capable in a managerial capacity, as one who makes shrewd, far-sighted plans, you may attain fame as an ingenious engineer, or an illustrious designer of fine catalogs or similar literature, as a financial genius—oh, you may be tops in so many occupations, yet without having the fervent drive powered by ego that makes one good at selling. Every man, looking at himself in the mirror of life, would do well to repeat that popular expression of the day to himself, "I've got to be me!"

On the flip side, it takes understanding of human nature, an inherent empathy, that instinctive sense of how it is to be in the other fellow's shoes, to help sense what will appeal to the prospect's minds. Which in turn brings up the nice guy image:

It may be true that in baseball, nice guys finish last but in the business world, we're not playing games. Now, I have no intention of writing a book on etiquette. If a man prefers to eat peas with his knife, I figure it's his prerogative to live as dangerously as he pleases. And so on. But in marketing, one important facet of the nice guy image is to remember how *suppressed* so many men are. That buyer who is the rep's objective, wants to indulge in natural feelings by expressing them—but he can seldom do that. For instance: in the presence of his boss, he must zip to the right—he *has* to respectfully listen. He can't just indulge in an intimate little chat here and there with his secretary because neither his boss or his wife approves of consorting with her other than as it concerns the prosaic bolts and nuts of their jobs.

And, speaking of his wife: talking in her presence also may present the hopelessness of contending with her feminine need to do the talking. His children—if they happen to be home when he is there and within hearing range at all, in this day and age very likely are at the point where they barely tolerate him, let alone listen.

So, ah!—along comes you. If *you*, then, being possessed of that empathy which makes you willing to be the good listener the poor guy so badly needs, you've got the makings of a friend. A rep who is able to supress his own entirely normal desire to do the talking but instead encourages the other fellow to relieve himself, is a salesman of distinction, the man most likely to succeed, the one who proves nice guys finish first. A few examples of commonly arising situations that call for self-restraint:

If your buyer friend makes a griping reference to the excessive charge made by a plumber who only changed the washers in his kitchen sink, agree that some repairmen overcharge nowadays instead of trying to beat him with the story of what a fortune it cost *you* to have a leak in your roof repaired. If he speaks of a fender-bender accident he had that morning, sympathize; don't try to outdo him with a dramatic recountal of how your car or somebody else's was totaled. Should he be suffering from the sneezing, eye-swollen, coughing of a bad cold, don't make his ailment sound inconsequential with a story of how you barely escaped catching tuberculosis.

In other words: a nice guy is one who allows the other fellow to be the champ in complaining about the exigencies of the day simply by being in compassionate agreement that he certainly does have cause to be aggrieved. A good salesman keeps recital of *his* troubles for someone trying to sell *him* something.

Make no mistake about ego; for a salesman, it's the same kind of consciousness of self that makes a man battle fiercely with all he's got to become president of the United States. Couple that with empathy, the kind exhibited by a doctor who has good bedside manners, and you're on your way home with the business signed, sealed and tucked away in your brief case, ready to be forwarded to your principal! □

21

WHAT PRICE THE SALES ENGINEER?

It's a meaningful term

The conjunction of "engineer" with "salesman," used as an occupational description, had a somewhat ludicrous origin. When the Korean situation hit the headlines in 1950, a worried electronic rep recalled the gas rationing of World War II. If war conditions developed and gas rationing was to be again introduced, he felt that as an "engineer" he might receive more favorable consideration in securing adequate allotments of gasoline than would a mere "salesman." He consequently concocted the term "sales engineer" and adopted it for business cards and letterhead. Though somewhat awkward-sounding at first, people became accustomed to it and its usage spread across the nation. Eventually, in view of its unlooked-for but very real application, it assumed a definite meaning in itself.

The business world often invents fanciful labels or terms to identify enterprises and people, but there probably has never been a commercial description devised that more accurately presents a man's vocation than "sales engineer" — that is, providing it is truly representative by nature of the industry or product category. That its correct application has been distorted by such mutations as "sanitation engineer" for street-sweeper or janitor and so on, is unfortunate but, for the sales manager seeking appropriate representation or for the salesman intent on clearly distinguishing his occupation, the use of "sales engineer" should be applied with understanding of its true significance.

The term is more meaningful than being merely a matter of semantics. The salesman calling on technical trade — the kind usually lumped up under "industrial" — is pretty apt in most cases to be really at least something of an engineer, or a reasonable facsimile thereof. If he doesn't actually have occasion to make his product presentation to engineers, he does have to be able to talk intelligently about it with the knowing buyer of industry's more complex technical products anyway. In such cases, "sales engineer" is a most appropriate designation.

All too often, the suitability of the term may be misrepresented. A rep lacking in technical expertise, although perhaps an experienced agent otherwise, entranced by visions of huge commissions to be made from a highly technical line that happens to be available, may solicit the line. The sales manager might be overly impressed by a voluble, personable individual, a glib proponent of his own worth. Carried away by urgent need to expedite coverage of an open territory, he appoints that applicant — a decision soon to be regretted, leading to early termination of the sales agreement, to be charged off as a costly experience to both parties.

The old saw to the effect that "a good salesman can sell anything" needs re-sharpening. It just ain't so — not in today's mechanical-electrical-electronic-space age. To sell one or a dozen or a gross of electric toothbrushes to the drug sundry trade may not require the special competence of an honestly termed "sales engineer" but to sell the parts that make them, does! In the latter case, in that rep's life, sales engineering is what he does most.

A unique anomaly in the philosophy of selecting salesmen was described by the sales manager of a retail home entertainment chain of stores recently while addressing a trade association meeting. He had been asked by someone in the audience of sales agents what he thought about the help of engineering competence in the salesman employed to sell technical merchandise — his products being, of course, technical in nature.

"If you're selling computers," he replied, "you need some degree of engineering expertise. But when we interview prospective salesmen to sell our radios, TV, CB and hi-fi outfits, we deliberately pass up the technicians, the experimenters, the hobbyists of the amateur radio operator type and the like — people who probably know more about the technology of our products than any of us in management. For our purposes, such people are too interested in the product's guts; they can't help but talk about what makes the things go.

"We like people preferably who are homebodies — who don't know and don't care other than to enjoy what the products do — just as envisioned by the customer. Give me a cheerful young music lover, of either sex or, say, an experienced furniture salesman, for instance, and I'll show you sales people who will sell a lot of the better kind of TV sets because they'll be talking about the good shows and how well they can be seen and heard and enjoyed — not about what's inside the cabinet. It's the old story — the sizzle rather than the steak. In our case, we sell entertainment rather than the means of reproducing it."

He made me think that if, similarly, the railroads had sold the places people go to rather than just tickets for getting there, they might not have been displaced to the point of bankruptcy by the various other means of transportation that developed. Of course that sales manager's shrewd appraisal of human nature is a philosophy applicable at the retail level of selling and, naturally, in any case, it is indeed desirable that the salesman be one of ebullient personality, enthusiastic, practiced in the social amenities that make readily for friendships.

However — where technical understanding is required — as

would be the case of a rep charged with selling those disdained "guts," i.e. the components for manufacturing those same entertainment products, technical proficiency becomes an important requisite. That being the case, in turn then, usage of the descriptive title "sales engineer" is desirable because it carries with it implications of authority, of special competence and, as such, the rep should be so described. It should appear on his stationery and should similarly be employed by the manufacturer in advertising, in his literature or wherever references may be made to his sales people.

For the rep's calling cards and likewise for his letterhead, the following graphic occupation description makes an all points covered format when printed under the company name:

MANUFACTURERS' $^{\text{sales}}_{\text{engineering}}$ REPRESENTATIVES

You may have difficulty restraining the printer's tendency to set copy in straight lines, without understanding the significance of this format. Explain to him that you want "sales" a half space *above* the main line ("manufacturers' representatives" being the "main" line), and to set "engineering" a half space *under* the main line. And, of course, its effectiveness is increased if you have MANUFACTURERS' REPRESENTATIVES printed in one color and "sales engineering" in another.   ☐

22

THE BEE GOES WHERE THE HONEY IS

A problem in arithmetic

The following discusses an approach to a major problem apparently contradicting what I have written previously on the subject of customer classification from the point of cold figures return. This is not a matter of inconsistency but is simply intended to bring out the other side of a subject which is admittedly controversial and on which only the rep himself can make a final decision. This time, I'm not promoting the practice of going out after small customers who, in the aggregate, might be more profitable than the beginners and who are easier to deal with than the big accounts. Instead, the desirability and/or methodical process of *eliminating* the small fry in order to concentrate on one's biggest customers, will be considered.

One observation before we get down to brass tacks: I am not going to tell you a thing you don't already know, to wit: that if you're not making money on a customer, who needs him? The point is, however, that for so many of us, the need to cut down the list of actual buying customers doesn't strike us as urgent; a euphoric "you never can tell" attitude restrains action or the procrastination may be simply because the subject just floats vaguely around in one's mind without receiving *the organized or systematic application it requires.* Just how costly may be your failure to act on the situation is something you will have to determine for yourself but, in the interests of efficiency and in the final analysis, what has to be evaluated is the relationship between your available manpower and the number of worthwhile calls your firm can make. It becomes something of a problem in arithmetic.

Excepting only the man who is determined for his own good and sufficient reasons to remain a one-man operation, no doubt every established rep wishes he could have more manpower. There are always lines that need deeper working because of potential for expansion, new prospective customers looming up, more lines that could be added to one's roster. Since putting on extra salesmen is not always practical, what can be done about more efficient use of the hands already on hand? Well, one way is to cut down on the number of people you call on.

The number of calls and their cost are factors which should be receiving the rep's most critical judgment. You're probably aware of figures ranging all the way out to eighty bucks cost per call and even more. In view of the variations in types of calls, I've never seen much point in trying to use figures purporting to present the average cost per call unless they stem from businesses which are in exact duplication of one's own. So much is dependent on the size of the firm and its corresponding overhead, quality of the calls made (such as length of time per call, for instance), the kind of product and form of selling required, the time differences in calls between those on prospective and on long established clientele, time consumed in traveling from one call to another, as well as special circumstances such as, for example, the presence of employees inside as backup for the outside men.

However, there is no reason why a rep can't calculate the cost of *his own* operation. No doubt you have your way of doing this but otherwise, just for the sake of simplification here, take your total cost of doing business per year and divide that by the total number of calls you and your staff made during that same period; that to be used as the cost of sales.

Say you average 5 calls per day per man and we'll assume you have 250 working days per year so that each of you makes a total of 1,250 calls per year. Each one of those calls absorbed some time and accounted for a proportionate part of your overhead expense. Total the amount of sales per customer, calculate how much commission you made on that sales total and subtract your cost of making that amount of sales. Then, set up a list for the past year of those customers and the figures just calculated.

Now, divide your customers into three brackets dollar-wise insofar as the commission you made on their last year's business is concerned. Call them "Profitable," "So-so" and "Poor." The first is self-explanatory, "So-so" means those on whom your commission came to something more than what your calls on them cost and "Poor" stands for those on whom your commissions only equalled or were less than your cost of calling on them.

The "Poor" list is the first and of course easiest to dispose of. You might want to hang on to an exceptional few because of some special potentialities such as, perhaps, contract negotiations in progress which in turn could bring you a desirable share of their business. No doubt there are a few you consider border-line, in which case you keep them on your prospect line, but set an estimate or limit on how many more calls to make on them until you can decide whether or not to continue looking upon them as "customers." For the rest, eliminate them from your lists of calls.

The tough one is going to be the "So-so" middle class. True, they are profitable to the extent that you received more in commission than your calls on them cost. But, *enough* for the time and effort involved? Could you have made *more* money for the same amount of time they consumed? What do knowledgeable members of your staff think? *Would it be preferable to give the middle class less attention, perhaps even eliminate these "So-so" accounts?* The bee does need a certain amount of time in order to get to where the honey is. Would the time saved on the "So-so" trade be used more profitably when applied to the high profit type of prospects?

Speaking of progress being impeded by deadwood: a rep friend of mine, employing several crack salesmen, had put a revised remuneration plan in effect. Without trying to cover all the details here: briefly, it made the salesmen personally responsible for their own calls by directing and scheduling themselves with the portion of the territory assigned to them. A drawing account was allowed but all forms of guarantee were discontinued. They were supplied with office space and secretarial service but otherwise were required to pay their own expenses.

Generous commissions or "splits" in the commissions were based on and limited to exactly the business they brought in. In short: they were in business for themselves. For this rep, the arrangement worked out beautifully. In each case, the man's sales volume increased as did his remuneration accordingly. A fringe benefit was that the men themselves, having intimate, personal knowledge of each customer, were able to do the job of weeding out the "Poor" and the "So-so" classes.

That led to such results as this: the rep noticed by the salesmen's call reports that a prominent company in particular, on whom one of the salesmen had been calling regularly once a week, no longer appeared on that man's list of calls. Likewise, no orders had ever been received from the subject company even though they were known to use items similar to those handled by this rep. After some quiet investigation, the rep learned that (a) all of the company's purchases were made from a central head office far removed from the rep's territory and that (b) the local man on whom the salesman had been previously calling was a bowling teammate of the salesman and the call was actually no more than a visit for discussion of their mutual sport interest! (With the situation now in effect having corrected itself, the rep chuckled to himself and refrained from throwing it up to his salesman. But what he did

*do was to persuade his principal to allow him commission on
the portion of the referenced company's purchases which
were shipped into the rep's territory!)*

I'm sure you're not going to take very kindly to the
heresy of dropping prospective customers, especially any
from whom you've had at least some business! Of course! it
goes against any good salesman's grain to give up a prospect
and I'm not necessarily suggesting that you should. But—the
nitty and the gritty of it is to take a good, *hard* look at your
lists, to force yourself into calculating just how much money
it costs to stay in contact, to send mailings, to make sales
calls, to continue with people from whom, over a reasonable
period of time, you did not receive enough business to pay
for your costs in continuing to treat them as prospective
customers. What I'm saying is: get yourself into the position
of being able to answer *mathematically* the question—just
where is the point of no return?—and with hard-nosed
determination, act accordingly.   □

23

YOU AND THE TELEPHONE COMPANY

For better communication efficiency at lower cost

Are you aware that the telephone company, i.e., the Bell System, American Tel & Tel and subsidiaries, have a market-ing philosophy, that they are concerned with you and me as customers? That they are aware of how big communication figures in business problems? That they believe they can be of help but that to solve your problems they have to understand them? And that they're willing — that they have what they call "Account Representatives," fully trained and ready to deal with your *problems of communication?*

And if you think the foregoing reads like one of the phone company's ads, you're quite perceptive. Most of the phraseology was actually cribbed from a Bell System ad. BUT — !

In the cynicism that so often overtakes us, we are apt to condemn such big factors in our lives as politicians and the phone company with about the same degree of vehemence — while unmindful that there is such a thing as a favorable side. Not all politicians are grafters, sluggards or sinners — there are those who actually are dedicated to working in the public interest. The telephone company is not out to gouge us down to the last phonecon but realizes that to stay in healthy financial and good political status (not the least, cast-ing a wary eye on the competition growing) they must do right by us. So — why not take advantage of their assistance — because it *is* there if you but *ask for it*.

It is apparent that the average rep doesn't know just how

much more efficient and economical his telephone system can be. At a recent meeting of an ordinarily very progressive rep association, with seventy-five in attendance, it turned out that only two men knew that the phone company actually had representatives trained and available to help design the best new communication system for a firm or to revamp one as it currently exists.

It is not simply a matter only of selected, appropriate equipment. For example:

The phone company will supply complete breakdown of telephone costs *per individual* within a rep firm. In the case of one fairly large firm, the company bills separately for each of fifteen individual phone lines. This includes each line on rotary service. The purpose of multiplicity of lines: internally, each department head is assigned a specific line or a line may be designated for some one special purpose such as, for example, outgoing calls to industrial distributors.

The billings from the individual lines are spread sheeted into a monthly report, to be read by all. If further clarification is required, the details are neatly broken down in a specific phone bill. Think of how much paperwork, of bookkeeping those billings supply ready made, neatly prepared for the rep owner and his staff to study. The phone company will even assign different credit card call numbers to each outside salesman, followed with itemizing *them* individually on their billings.

For extensive users of the telephone, the WATS line has to be a bargain for the 10 hours metered use when you consider that billing is based upon six-second intervals. One rep claims to have tripled his phone time for his same costs previously using direct dial phone to principals.

Another possible savings is in "foreign exchange" usage for your local area. If your office is, say, 20 to 50 miles from a major market area, you can save on message unit calls by buying a "foreign exchange" within the active territory, thus lowering the message unit usage. Various fitting ar-rangements of the best system for you have to be studied and an analysis made of your phoning patterns and present costs. As the Bell System ad says, "No single person has the knowledge and experience to deal with the problems of every business. So we have aligned our efforts on an industry-by-industry basis . . . each divion has an in-depth understanding of the problems faced by its customers. The heart of each is an Account Representative who is assigned to you."

Too many manufacturers' sales reps have a way of staying with phone systems rapidly becoming antiquated while that industry is exploding with new and better service. Even phonovision is in sight—no pun intended!—as a not-too-distant possibility for the everyday phone user. If you haven't had a telephone company representative go over your system within at least the past two years, you may be losing much in the way of both money and communication efficiency. All you have to do is call your phone company and set up the appointment. The result may repay you many times over. □

24

KEEPING PRINCIPAL AND
CUSTOMER APART

Sometimes best for all concerned

Something about which a manufacturers' representative
develops ambivalent feelings is the uncertainty of what will
result when one of his principals and a customer are in
direct communication. If there is anything which gives an
experienced rep a sense of foreboding, it is the prospect of
customer and principal getting together without him present — unless the contact is deliberately instigated by the rep
at the proper time. If you ask me — I have the scars to prove
the need for such concern!

Let's first eliminate the obvious that would indicate the
contrary of that avowal. At the trade shows, it *is* customary
and *is* most desirable that customers meet the factory personnel. Indeed, yes! When sales managers or other factory
people come into your territory on field trips, in most cases
it *is* of value to take them around to call on selected
customers and — with certain reservations to be discussed
later — can be most beneficial to all concerned.

Also, we'll dispose of worrying about possible boo-boos
perpetrated by your visiting fireman, of being uneasy because the factory man doesn't know the customer the way
you do. Being familiar with what the buyer prefers and dislikes, you wouldn't necessarily lie but you would manage
to avoid getting mucked up in sticky subjects whereas your
sales manager might not know better. It's all too easy to
innocently touch on a raw nerve when you don't know your

man. But—that isn't too terrible, either. Presumably you would anticipate and prepare your sales manager for any specific hazards in prospect during a customer facing.

Of course, there are exceptions—unfortunately, more than one might think—of sales managers who, arrogant in their sense of power, leave much to be desired in the way of normal deference or courtesy to the man who puts out the orders. I recall one sales manager (I don't dare describe him, even indirectly—too many people would recognize him) who was noted for exceeding reasonable limits in the use of profanity. His typical greeting when, perforce, I had to haul him around to visit certain customers whom he had met previously, was an unpunctuated "Well, hello you sonofabitch how are you?", his subsequent conversation heavily interlarded with four-letter wording. The supposed innocuous salutation and its allusion to his listener of dubious ancestry, might be accepted with a sickly smile as intended humor by the person addressed, but I writhed inside, knowing how I would have to explain and apologize for him after he was gone. (In fact, I was told of a situation in another territory, where two distributors admonished the local representative to keep that man off their premises.) But how about when the rep isn't present at a time of interchanges between principal and customer?

I once had a heart-stopping example of the havoc that can be wrought by a factory man in the case of one who took it upon himself to pass over the rep by communicating directly with the trade. It came within inches of a tremendous damage suit for libel, with my principal caught dead to rights. I can still shudder, remembering that awful experience.

An impatient-voiced Mr. G., the Research Chief for a certain internationally known corporation, with one of their most important laboratories in my city, had phoned me one morning to ask a question about a component manufactured by one of my principals that, he said, was part of a machine manufactured for them for many years. He explained shortly that a new possible usage had developed for their machines, involving the necessity of functioning in below-zero temperatures and would the referenced component stand up okay under these conditions?

I had nothing about sub-zero temperature characteristics in my files so I told him I'd obtain the information for him from my principal. As I learned later, Mr. G, typical of some engineers who look upon sales people with disdain and miffed because I couldn't give him the desired information off the top of my head, assumed that as a salesman I would probably drag or be entirely remiss in getting the required data with dispatch. Without telling me, that same day he addressed a repeat of the question to the factory, accompanying his letter with a drawing of the machine. His letter asked for a prompt reply.

Upon receiving my communication, and in the same mail its duplication and drawing from Mr. G., the factory's sales manager, treating the question as simply routine, passed it along to one of their rather new young engineers. That eager beaver, after giving the drawing his profound, learned study and noting the seeming rush requirements, thinking he would conserve the executive's time, took it upon himself to answer Mr. G. directly. He didn't even bother to send me a copy of his response. I had no warning before the bomb dropped.

Something of how San Francisco's residents felt when they had the 1906 earthquake, hit me. It started with a phone call from the president of a local customer of ours, of which I could only make out yelling commands for me to get my ass down there to his office and on the double! A while later, standing at bewildered attention in his office, I blinked at the roaring barrage, my eardrums blasted by an outpour of profanity, condemning the stupidity of my principal, of demanding to know what in the hell right they had to communicate with *his* customer over *his* head, and what did they mean by telling *his* customer the particular component they had been using for so many years, as originally specified by this blip-blip-bonehead factory, was a wrong model, that it should have been a different number—all of which had me staring with open-jawed mystification as the tragic facts emerged.

This O.E.M., who had been our customer for many years, had been supplying an assembly incorporating the component in question to that Research Engineer's company, to function as a major section of the company's completed machine. It evolved that Mr. G.'s company was a customer of *our* customer, that our factory had indeed gone over *our* customer's head to *his* customer, that we *had* condemned our customer's judgment in using that particular component even though it had been particularly specified as the part to use by its manufacturer. Hundreds of the equipments were installed all over the world, some in most remote, hard to reach locations. My principal's young engineer, by writing Mr. G. as he did, had not only been insulting in impugning the judgment of our customer in employing that particular component. The horrible worst of it was that he had proclaimed it should be replaced with another number of *his* specification, which he pontifically declared was the proper one that should have been used in the first place!

Mr. G. naturally exploded. He had called our customer supplier's president to read him the devastating letter and the riot act, repeating again and again that his superiors were certainly going to hear about it. I couldn't get a word in edgewise as the president painted the horrifying specter of having to recall the innumerable machines produced over the years, that would now have to be worked over, many to be hauled back from far off corners of the world! Wildly gesticulating, shouting, he told me he was instructing his attorney to start a damage and libel suit at once! I finally managed to stammer out enough words for a holding action, to the effect that I would get in instant touch with my people — and staggered out.

Fortunately, I was able to reach my sales manager immediately, a man who stood only five feet three in height but, reminiscent of the world's famous short stature figures — the Stalins, the Churchills, the Steinmetzs, the Napoleons and other such shorties — he was a terrific man in action. At first, as he grasped my hot details of the tragic story, he'all but lost consciousness. However, when the blood started flowing again, he charged into action. I learned later of what followed:

First, he fired the engineer. Then he phoned the agitated Mr. G, to convince him beyond question that the part used for so long was absolutely the correct choice, that no other would serve a well, that it had been tested for temperature conditions many years ago, that the stupid engineer hadn't bothered to get their own data out of the files — which he was looking at right then and there, the tests proving that the subject component was fully capable of standing up under sub-zero conditions, that he would personally fly right out there and let Mr. G. see that data for himself. That took care of Mr. G.

A moment after that conversation, he called our customer's irate president to repeat what he had done, that Mr. G. was now fully satisfied and all was well with him again. In the final analysis, the saving grace was, of course, that there had been no instance of the part failing from any cause through all the years of its use. Which ultimately placated the customer and we all resumed breathing normally again.

That was just one graphic example of what can happen when a principal and the trade get into personal contact without benefit of the rep acting as their catalyst. Had I been smart back in those days (Lordy, how long it takes!), I would have probably forestalled the uproar by making certain I was convincing in assuring Mr. G. at the first contact that I would, indeed, personally take care of his problem, but pronto. In that event, the engineer would have sent his answer to *me*, I would have questioned his puzzling dictum because of knowing that the subject component had never given any trouble, to once again prove that an ounce of prevention is worth many long distance, nerve-wracking curative phone calls.

The possibilities for unfavorable consequences to all concerned when the rep isn't sitting in between principal and customer may arise from a number of angles. A common situation is not only when factory assistance with a technical problem is required, as in the previous incident, but perhaps a potentially big order is in prospect, calling for special pricing from management. The mistake occurs when the rep, trying to save time (or a sizable toll charge on his phone bill!) arranges for his prospect to be in direct phone communication with the key man at the factory.

If the problem is technical and gets solved, the rep has to be told about it at second-hand — very likely by the customer — and then can only flutter about, a sort of hang-dog figure. Which isn't conducive to his standing with either the customer or the principal. And, it is possible he may not actually have learned how to handle the problem himself, should it come up again. If at all possible, as my hindsight now indicates, of course his best bet would be to *himself* obtain the answers, in turn to pass them on, — thus making *him* the hero.

Now, suppose it is special pricing. Excited by the size of the order in sight, prompted by one thing or another, the prospective big buyer is put on the phone to discuss it with the factory's sales manager and they hold a bargaining session to which the rep is not privy. The prospect talks big numbers. The sales manager is impressed. He responds with a particularly low price — and takes the order.

Result? The buyer now feels he no longer needs the representative, that hereafter he'll do better dealing directly with the factory. The sales manager, perhaps deprecating the work done by the rep in building up the prospect's interest in the product, sounds off on how *he* got the big order. The question arises, at least by inference: who needs the rep? Obviously, the rep should extract his principal's rock-bottom price himself and, thus armed, go after the order, to nail it down on his own.

Then you have the kind of situation where the buyer is known *to you* to be a practicing chiseler, but not to the sales manager. Let me tell you of such an incident when a New York manufacturer, headed up by an old friend of mine, had written to ask if I would help out in making a market test for a new razor blade they had designed, of which all back there thought very highly. If things looked promising for its future and if they were to go ahead with it, perhaps I would like to take it on for the California territory? They had just made a small production run, only enough for samples in doing the research: the question was what would be the chances for a new razor blade in a very competitive market, completely unknown, carrying no big advertising, but of excellent quality and priced very low? Would the trade go for it?

I made a few exploratory calls. The regular drug sundry distributors weren't enthused about taking on an off-brand, no-name product, but they didn't say positively. It was going to take a lot of hard, tough selling, but not at all an impossible situation. I turned tentatively to one of the well known chains of discount stores, figuring a razor blade priced at half that of the leading brands might be just a natural for them. It would be interesting to get their reaction.

The purchasing agent tossed the sample blade I had handed him back on his desk with a scornful gesture. "Hell's fire, Buddy—there was a guy came through here a few weeks ago with that same blade. You're quoting me $2.00 a carton? His price was $1.50—you trying to get rich on me?"

It was difficult to restrain my desire to laugh in his face. Not only did I know he couldn't possibly be aware of the blade's existence before I called on him with it but I readily recognized the familiar old opening line used in the practice of chiseling, to which I had been introduced long before in dealing with masters of that art. I was also secretly pleased, knowing that *by the very act of starting to haggle*, he had revealed interest in what I had to sell.

> *Way back in my first youthful experience in business for myself, I had operated a battery shop in the heart of L.A.'s used car dealers' area—they being the notorious horse-traders of the 1920s. Those were the days when it was common practice to load the transmissions of the beat-up old clunkers they had for sale on their lots with bits of cork and the crank-cases were filled with the heaviest of oil, practically grease — shenanigans employed to quiet the machine's clatter when being demonstrated to a possible buyer. Another trick they used on me until I finally caught up and thereafter refused to cooperate was to have one of my service batteries installed (at a rental of twenty-five cents a day) while the car was being shown and, soon as sold, replacing it with the car's old junk battery which was probably ready to fall apart.*
>
> *As for if, as and when they had to actually put out the money to buy a battery (heaven forbid!) or found it necessary to pay me to repair one, the clamor, the storming and wailing, the bargaining voice raised over mine with claims of being robbed blind would go on and on, eventually to wear me down and I would finally give in just to have an end to the haggling, depite learning they were automatically putting me through their performances because they considered that good business.*

As I indicated back there a ways, time smartens us up. So when that chain store p.a. off-handedly asked for the name of the blade manufacturer's president, pretending he knew him but just happened to have momentarily forgotten the name, I "forgot" it, too—and changed the subject. I was pretty certain that if he knew the name of someone of importance at the factory, the fame of the chain as big operators and talking big numbers would get him a quotation at a particularly lower than regular price, since the factory would be favorable to getting production going with a nice fat order. He would place his order, get the blades in and would advertise the item at a deeply cut-rate price. Knowing their tactics I felt they would be using it as a leader, which would have ruined the territory for me right in the beginning. Retreating with a pleasant adieu, thus keeping this outfit temporarily out of our picture, until I got the product started with three regular distributors (space doesn't permit but that was a story in itself!) that same chain later became a good customer, buying at our standard pricing.

It is only good business from the standpoint of both principal and agent, to operate through the rep. That's what he's paid for. The principal doesn't know the buyer as the rep does—that the prospect may be a habitual chiseler, that he only talks big numbers but buys small, that his company's credit is beginning to show signs of wearing thin—just a variety of meaningful conditions bearing on the possibility of a big order being placed that, in all good practice, should have the principal leaving it to the rep to handle the situation properly. (As I've said many times, if he can't trust the rep, he'd better replace the guy!)

In any event, it's poor judgment for the same manager to denigrate his reps by placing himself in front of them. Making them look inconsequential in the trade's eyes weakens them and serves to reflect unfavorably upon himself.

The Chiseler. As a kind of postscript to this chapter: referring to mention of "the chiseler," a bit of bolts-and-nuts discussion about this most irritating crack in the glass and his routines may not be amiss. I'm speaking of the buyer who just automatically lapses into bargaining for a lower price than quoted—often not really expecting to get concessions but is motivated from force of habit, a game, a way of life. Even though he sits in a sumptuous, rare-wood panelled office, at a finely finished hardwood desk and surrounded by ornate furnishings, nevertheless no matter what you quote, this buyer may use smoother language but he haggles over the pricing like an itinerant sidewalk street peddler.

In the first place—and this is true of all but one kind of sales presentation—one should try to avoid being derailed by talking about price—the exception being where low price would be the product's most important feature. A good salesman will try to confine himself to stressing quality, usefulness, convenience, color—whatever the features of the product may be—until, finally, and to be disposed of as lightly as possible, you come to the price.

But, having followed that procedure, now you have a prospective buyer who determinedly seizes upon the subject of price, starting with a disdainful, "You're too high."

You naturally respond with, "Not too high for a product that—" and you repeat the main attractive features. If he dismisses that with a "Yes, but—," thereby acknowledging, even by inference, that he is impressed with the worthiness of your product, simply hold your ground. Explain *why* the product is priced as quoted—the high price of the skilled labor to manufacture it, the quality built in—etc., etc.

In some cases, you already know your man, that this buyer's response, no matter what price he is given, will be to haggle and try to beat you down. Of course, an old but in some cases the most effective method, is to quote a price at first higher than what you are willing to sell for, by way of anticipating his attack, giving you leeway to come down to the real price.

Or, another approach is to withhold information about freight allowances, extra cash discount terms, etc., to be used as a "concession" to meeting his demand for lower pricing.

Finally—suppose you've offered your absolutely lowest price. He continues to haggle. You simply close the book on him with a firm, "Sorry, my friend, but that's it—the best I can do. So—how about it? You sign here—on this dotted line." If he *is* impressed with your product and *can* use it to his advantage, in the face of your determination and if he was only bluffing on being able to do better with your competition, you will walk out with the order.

Which is your name of the game. □

25

BINGO CARDS AND THE
YAWNING ROUND FILE

Treatment of bounce-backs

I'm afraid some of my rep friends will greet this with raised eyebrows, even with imprecations, accusing me of being a traitor to the cause. However, what's right is right and I'm going to have my say — namely, that there are some reps who carelessly or more likely in ignorance fail to consider all the implications and potentialities inherent in those magazine enclosed enquiry cards, commonly called "bingo cards," and similar information requests received by their principals and passed on to the cognizant reps. Surprisingly enough, while not too many, there are far more than there should be who are not only remiss in their duties to their principals but short-sighted in their own interests when they preemptively select only those enquiry names that they recognize at a glance and contemptuously toss the rest away.

It's those "rest" that we're concerned with. The professional rep who knows what he is doing always looks upon these "unknowns" as possible gold mines and stakes out his claims accordingly. It isn't too difficult to definitely determine which of these enquiries might be very much worth following up — rather than to be discarded without further attention as the case might be.

For the moment, let's agree that any rep who isn't a damned fool realizes thar's gold in them thar hills of bingo cards and other written inquiries. The principal has been spending substantial money to advertise his products in *trade publications* in order to dig up those precious bits of prospective wealth, aiming his efforts specifically at *those who are members of his particular industry.* It obviously follows, then, that the *readership* of said publications is made up of people with whom *the rep in that industry identifies.*

Among those readers are possible customers. How many? At this point, we don't know. But, if a reader has taken the time and trouble to fill out a bingo card and mail it in, or has used his own stationery and paid the postage to write a note of inquiry requesting information about the advertisers' products, we have prima facie evidence he *must* have *some* need for what that information is to tell him. To determine what that need is, should make him a man of a certain amount of distinction in the cognizant rep's life.

If I were a sales manager, I would make mighty sure that the rep knows the calculation which sales managers all probably make, or certainly should, and that is dividing the number of inquiries received into the cost of the company's magazine advertising, to thus arrive at an evaluation of what the "bingo card" or similar inquiry costs *per each.* To secure such inquiries isn't the only purpose of the advertising, of course, but base the point on that figure in order to graphically impress the rep with the fact that such inquiries call for top priority attention. But — well — how much and to what extent "attention?"

As a rep shuffles through a newly received batch of inquiries, he of course will immediately recognize and remove selectively those which look like good leads for immediate follow-up and those which he does actually know are worthless. That is: of the latter, one kind he would be justified in immediately tossing into the wastepaper basket would be the literature requests from people known to him to be afflicted with clippititus — (there really should be such a word!) — meaning guys who clip coupons, who are only literature collectors, known from previous experience to be unconscionable time wasters. They vary in kind.

I remember one bingo card follow-up which turned out to be a young fellow draftsman working for a major customer in our area who, I found, lived alone in a one-room apartment, surrounded by huge dust-collecting accumulations of catalogs piled up all over the place. He was quite brazen — not at all abashed to admit he collected these in order to use pictures from them as models from which he practiced sketching, planning some day to leave his employer's drawing board to become a commercial illustrator!

That leaves us with the in-between — the unknown. What do you do about them — efficiently, without using up valuable time needlessly?

Those "unknowns" cost the principal, per each, just as did those which were immediately recognized. Does one find gold lying on the surface, without calling for digging to extract it? There are two simple ways to follow up. One, the phone: the other, via the mails. The latter is the quickest, and easiest, though not necessarily the better of the two. You simply keep on hand a form letter to be mailed to the person making the inquiry which tells him you have become aware of his interest, that you represent this manufacturer and asking what you can do in the way of serving him. With that letter you enclose an addressed, postage-paid card to be filled out for entering the addressee's requirements, with a box to be checked indicating when you may call on him, etc. That's perfunctory, but for some it may be considered enough.

Better than that — *far* better — is to call the key individual on the phone, introduce yourself as the rep for that particular line. Ask a few leading questions whose answers will indicate to you whether or not to follow with a personal call or to drop in at that point. Or — another way to do it:

Perhaps you are one of those reps who is a favorite of Heaven and that therefore, you may be graced with a *good* secretary. Oh, man — lucky you! In that blessed event, train her to make the phone call for you — not only to conserve your time but to impress the prospective customer. How train her? Make up a scenario with her part in the script to read something on this order, with the actual wording and questions worked up to fit your operation; she calls the man who made the inquiry:

"Good morning, Mr. E. This is the Harold Repper Company — I'm Mr. Repper's secretary. He had to be out this morning so he asked me to reply to you about this inquiry of yours — which you mailed recently to the ZYX Co., whom we represent in this area" (Note — "reply" — to forestall having him jump to the conclusion that this is a random soliciting phone call.)

Once Mr. E. has recalled the bingo card or letter he wrote, he may make a vague rejoinder — something about "just happened to read their ad — " She persists.

Secretary: "Do you have any requirements that Mr. Rep could take up with you — now or at some future time?"

Even if he says No, he's going to *have* to come up with *some* kind of justification for making his inquiry — which in itself can be revelatory, with, say, something like an allusion to a prospective project coming up. Her aim should be to get him talking. He may reply in the affirmative, perhaps Yes, now — or at some future time. If "now" or "soon," she says she will advise Mr. Repper accordingly but she will have to check his agenda to ascertain when he may call. At this point and especially if he is offhand about when he would want to discuss the matter further, she is in a position to elicit *some* meaningful preliminary information (assuming he has not come out with a strong No, not interested):

Secretary: "By the way, Mr. E — I'm sure Mr. Repper must know your company but, just for my own interest — have you been in business a long time? . . . Oh really? . . . What kind of things do you make? . . . My, is that so! That's interesting! Do you have a lot of people working there? . . . I see

. . . Incidentally, when Mr. Repper calls, do you have different buyers for various departments? Whom should he see?"

Such leading conversation, even though brief, should do much to reveal what kind of outfit was responsible for the inquiry — what they do, how big they may be, the possible degree of interest in your products — all stemming from just a few, well worded questions.

Obviously, the rep himself could make that call and in many cases I suppose he would or perhaps should. Each must decide for himself whether to phone and do his own probing, or turn it over to his secretary — having in mind however, in the latter case as I indicated above, she be a *good secretary*. If having no histrionic abilities, and if she would be the kind who would just mechanically ask the indicated questions as though reading the words instead of saying them on her own, forget it! Do it yourself!

Also, if you have male help in your office, the same part can be assigned accordingly, to act out just as well — in some cases perhaps better. The main point is (a) that you check out *every* inquiry and (b) that you dig out all the usable info beforehand that you can for which the phone is so well suited and, finally — now don't get mad at me, fellows — I know from personal experience how irritating this can be: though no one has complained more than I have about selfish, demanding principals who are unreasonable in their demands for voluminous written call reports, I think you should somehow make a kind of report, if necessarily brief, of what happened following your receipt of a number of inquiries sent to you by your principals. I'll explain later why this can be important to you yourself as well as to your principal. In the meantime there are simple, time-conserving ways to do this chore — and incidentally to help placate sales managers who demand extensive reports covering your calls:

Have a form made up — standardized — just for factory reports. (Easy to do. Type it once—have a printer "instant" reproduce it—inexpensive 8½ by 11 paper—will do the job.) Head it: FOLLOW UP OF PROSPECT INQUIRIES. Date it as may be called for and check off each inquiry on it, something on this order:

1. JRX CO. Called on buyer. Quotations requested. Very promising. 2. James Blow: A coupon clipper—wastes everybody's time. Lead returned herewith to cancel from your records. 3. Clows, Inc. Planning for some vague, distant future. Seems legitimate but a long time off. Will see again in a couple of months. 4. General Co. Man who made inquiry gone. His replacement says, see him after he has settled down. Will do.

And so on. These may or may not be extensive enough to be considered call reports but are to be passed on to the principal's advertising department for guidance in proving just how effective or not is the advertising they have been putting out for. Your principal *will* be grateful for your comments. After all, the extent to which his advertising is effective certainly affects you, and if you can help him determine where he does or does not get good results for his advertising dollar, you are helping to prove you are not just an ordinary would-be order taker but an important part of the team.

If you are conscientious in checking out those "unknowns," you are liable to get some real surprises. For instance: very often, someone who is really an important person for the rep to know, is really with a sizable company—but he sends in an inquiry under his individual name without giving the company name, the response to be addressed to his home. I often encountered that situation. Why?

Sometimes, it would be because he is planning to leave that company and is going to branch out on his own—therefore he wants certain catalogs and so on but doesn't want his departure to become known until he's ready to resign. Another may be because of poor internal distribution—if it's literature, it gets kicked around at the point of receipt and the addressee doesn't receive it. I'd hate to mention a certain famous airplane manufacturer—notorious for losing employee mail to a point where, by their men's own instructions, I had sometimes like a couple dozen on our mailing list who had instructed us to send our material to them at their home addresses rather than to the plant, to be sure the items would be received.　　　　　　　　　　　　　　　　　□

26

PUBLICIZE!

A sales agency is no place for a shrinking violet

Every time your name receives favorable or even nominal mention in print, it's like a deposit in the bank, because it makes your reputation as somebody *grow, to compound interest— in you, that is.*

I find it difficult to understand the neglect and apathy of reps who strive mightily to enhance importance of themselves in their respective industries—with the sales managers, the customers—in shortsightedly continuing to overlook the priceless value of "getting your name in print." To attain stature in your industry, to achieve country-wide recognition, that identification which has you standing out from the hoi polloi, can be approached in large degree by continual issuance of "publicity releases" and/or by engaging in activities calculated to make you a public figure. It's not all that difficult.

I have known reps with plenty of self-confidence, with expanded egos who, for some reason or other mystifying to me, are diffident about seeing their names publicized if it has to be instigated by themselves. They excuse reluctance to publicize themselves by sneering at contemporaries wise in the ways of getting publicity, charging them with putting out a lot of claptrap. They choose to overlook the basic fact that trade publications report activities of people in their particular industries in order to draw the advertising which keep them in existence. It should be manifest that the publishers *have* to have news about persons whose activities in some way or other may be of interest to various or all segments of the industry to which they cater. They welcome "press releases."

The fact that a rep is announcing a move to larger quarters is an indication of progress and as such, to the editors, can constitute usable "news." If the rep has become an official of some civic committee or has taken on an important officership in his trade association, is celebrating his 25th wedding anniversary, has made a notable addition to his sales staff, was just appointed regional representative for some nationally known line, recently returned from a luxury cruise in foreign waters, has incorporated his business so that employees can share in its ownership, etc., etc., etc., — such is the fuel that keeps most of the trade publications alive and in business.

While not exactly to the point here, I can't help but relate an absurd anecdote told to me that, nevertheless, illustrates the principle of publicizing oneself:

> *A rep whose office and home were located in a small town centered in his territory, subscribed to a Chinese newspaper which, of course, he could not read. He knew his town and how gossipy it was, that from the circulating, gabby postmaster out, the distinction would make him a man who would stand out and be highly respected for his supposed erudition. In fact, when someone nominated him for a county committee, he was not only elected without opposition but was immediately chosen as its chairman!*

I have often heard reps say disgustedly, "I've tried that. I've spent a lot of money on stationery and postage, sending out p.r. without ever seeing a word of it in print." I don't doubt it. In most cases, such reps haven't taken the trouble or the time to learn just how the publicity copy should be drawn up. Again — that isn't too difficult. You don't have to be a professional advertising man to get up such copy, although if your capital will support it, that's the way to go — but you *can* do it yourself, with a little study.

It is only necessary to observe a few simple rules and — if I may be forgiven one of my favorite words, employ *empathy* — put yourself in the editor's place and consider what rafts of material he must receive that might be used in his publication but that he has to function under strict limitations with the space available. Therefore, aside from its possible news value, he is quick to judge the copy for being put together in the way they have to have it — otherwise loses no time tossing it out.

I am not going to enter into all the details of how to draw up "publicity releases" — there are books on that subject alone — but here are a few fundamentals, their observance enough to get you by in most cases:

1. Use 8½ by 11" standard paper. Type! Double Space! Don't try to do anything fanciful — this is no place for employing elaborate graphics. Leave one and a half to two inches of margin on both sides! If your copy consists of more than one page, leave three or four inches of space at the top of the front page. Be sure to say "continued, next page" or "more" at the lower right hand corner of the first page, and at the top of the next page type in "Page 2, continued from Page 1." At the end of your copy, insert the figure 30, which is the journalist's age-old sign that the "story" is finished, or type a couple of # symbols to represent finish, or just say "End." In the upper right hand corner, type "Contact" and follow with the name of the individual, address and phone number to reach in the event it becomes necessary to question somebody about the "release."

Pictures can be very helpful if they are good — but don't

send ordinary snapshots. No color pictures (too difficult and costly to reproduce). Supply sharp, glossy black and white prints, no smaller than 5" by 7" and preferably 8" by 10". A group photograph isn't looked upon with favor unless it is the very assembly of people itself that is the subject of the "news." Such photographs would have to be very large for features to be distinguishable, and the editor is always conscious of his space limitations.

Try to set out the major parts of your news in the first one or two paragraphs — the who-what-where-when of the story (keeping in mind that three lines of typing occupy one column inch of newspaper print). Here again, try to follow the editor's thinking. Suppose he doesn't consider your story all that great but is newsworthy enough for him to use some of it. Or—even if he would like to use the entire article, it just so happens that he doesn't have that much space available. So—he's going to chop your "news report" to make it fit into the "hole" he has designated for it. Therefore, consider what you would most like to have appear as he cuts off part of your copy, keeping that which is most important well up toward the beginning of it.

And finally, don't try to be foxy and get into your copy anything that smacks of advertising whatever you have to sell. Editors are quick to spot and delete such wording and consequently apt to throw out the whole thing. If you want to advertise — they have space for sale! One of the best things you can do is make a practice of reading publicity in the trade publications you receive—you'll soon learn what editors do consider acceptable for them to publish and can guide yourself accordingly.

The Publicity Picture

For reasons beyond me, even some of our long established, professional sales people overlook the importance of having good pictures on hand for publicity purposes, as well as to send principals—and even when they do, they so frequently exhibit a complete lack of imagination, of empathy. How often have you seen insipid photographs in newspapers and trade publications with the subjects of the articles looking vapidly, self-consciously or grimly into the camera, some with all but a frowning expression. In groups, they can look like a band of guerrillas ready to start a revolution or, if they are actually smiling, one must conclude it is only because the governor has just phoned his forgiveness, thus saving them from the firing squad.

A number of reasons exist to justify giving the subject of publicity pictures serious thought, not at all apparent at first glance. That they may be needed to assist in getting some publicity about your firm into the financial pages of newspapers (that kind of paper not being very conducive to good reproduction) should make it self-evident that the picture be of good quality and the subject properly posed. Incidentally, an important use for an attractive portrait study of "the headman," or "associates," the latter sometimes in action, can be helpful when it accompanies solicitation for a new line. Prospective principals are very much interested in what the people who are going to represent them look like. Another possible use for such photos is when you or members of your staff serve on trade associations or civic committees that may be publicized. And of course, if you make mailings to prospective customers, very often the copy is of a nature that could employ personalized pictures to advantage.

About costs and such: if you are going to use a professional photographer, he won't come cheap but, if he's good, he might be worth it. *If* he's good! Like in any occupation— there are variations in degrees of skill, whatever may be the charges for it. In my town, a certain "studio" photographer, with much claim to artistry, charges $30 to $50 for a simple portrait shot. A photography supply shop a few blocks away, will take your picture in a carton-strewn room in back of the main store for $5.00 and do a better job of it than the self-proclaimed "artist." He's got commercial sense!

In selecting your photographer, the one who takes those adorable baby pictures or dreamy reproductions of the bride, may be all right for such visionary work, but is he minded to do sharp black-and-white commercial work? *Ask to see samples.* Since photography is so popular and all kinds of fine equipment is now readily available for amateurs, there are many who go in for this fascinating hobby, who become quite skilled at it. Among them may be a friend of yours who would welcome the opportunity to practice on you for the nominal costs of the materials or you buy him a lunch — or sumpin.'

If your friend takes over the assignment and knows pretty well what is wanted, he will use black and white film only. Color pictures are out for publicity purposes. He will focus sharply, process for very contrasty results, the prints on glossy paper in order to reproduce well. Since your friend has bought a roll of film for this special job and since its cost is nominal, use up the roll. Don't stop at one or two shots. So often, a good picture is spoiled by just some one little defect. Repeat shots with variations in camera settings and pose angles until the roll is used up, so that you will have a number of choices.

If you're considering using pictures to send principals, don't limit your subject matter. Take shots of individuals, at their desks, phoning, holding conferences, in the warehouse, loading up in front of your building, and of the building itself, getting into your car with your briefcase held in prominent view and so on — human interest stuff. If your secretary is a good looker, by all means take advantage of that. There's nothing like a picture of a pretty girl to attract attention. This being for business purposes, no cheesecake, of course. Observing decorum, one pose might be of her at work, with her head turned back smiling over her shoulder into the camera — as though she were being interrupted at her work but smiles while she's doing it.

When you have a good variety of shots picturing personnel and in surrounding working conditions, try making up a montage of these scenes, laying them out to be reproduced on one 8½" by 11" page. Such a sheet might be useful to send to prospective principals and as a mailer for the trade.

As a staid businessman, you're pretty much bound by convention to use a formal head-shoulders-chest portrait of yourself, a dignified person, looking pleasantly into the camera. On the other hand, for other purposes, such as for prospective principals and mailings to customers, all it takes is a little imagination to make interesting pictures, keeping in mind that your subjects should look alive, in action, as opposed to stiff, formal, family album kind of portraiture. □

27

THE EMBARRASSMENT OF
ASKING FOR MONEY DUE YOU

You've ploughed, you've planted — why shouldn't you reap?

> *If money is due you — and it isn't forthcoming when it was supposed to — shouldn't you ask for it? Demand it?*
> *The subject of being embarrassed in asking for your money is one thing. However, the very mention of "embarrassment," just the word in itself, can be used helpfully when you are awaiting commissions considerably overdue.*

First, suppose you have the situation — common enough, as those who have been long repping know — of becoming concerned about commission you have been expecting which you should have received long ago. Most legitimate manufacturers nowadays function punctiliously by the calendar, taking care of obligations according to specific, periodic dates. Certainly employees are paid regularly — exactly by the week, the 15th of the month or in some cases on a monthly basis. One can visualize what would happen if the checks were late — trouble! — real trouble for that employer, eh? Direful strikes have been brought on for much less!

So why shouldn't sales reps be paid according to a fixed, dependable date? Doesn't the rep have *his* bills to meet, just as the direct employee has? Even more so — with his fixed costs of doing business — rent, phone, gasoline, secretaries, sales people, taxes, traveling expenses and a variety of fringe costs of doing business — to say nothing of his personal living expenses.

Independent sales representation doesn't exist on an investment of capital in stock, as in the merchandising sense — TIME is the rep's capital. And for the employment of that time, he is dependent on meeting his costs of doing business from his commissions. Since the nature of the business is such that seldom is the firm's bank balance much larger than the commissions received during a preceding month, it follows that a rep usually operates pretty close to the line. If his commission checks don't come through as expected, he can be facing trouble.

The unfortunate part of it is: the need to pay reps, in many cases, doesn't weigh as heavily on the principal's conscience as does the law which governs his obligation to pay salaries to his regular employees. If for any reason the principal is short of cash when the rep's commission is due, it is all too easy for him to simply postpone payment of the referenced amount at his own will. He figures the rep is going to be diffident about asking for his money, afraid of offending someone at the factory for fear of losing the line, that it is *embarrassing* to ask — and usually, he is right on all scores.

An overdue commission check is not only a matter of concern for the rep who needs the money to meet current obligations. If the stalling is really caused by the principal being in financial straits, the imminent possibility in prospect of the rep collecting whatever is due him if the principal goes bankrupt, makes it imperative that he get his money when due or at least not *too* long thereafter. Sad to say, when it comes to listing a bankrupt's creditors, as I once wrote, the rep is still pretty much the bottom man on the totem pole.

The following is quoted from a note received under date of December 20, 1976, from the "Congressional Research Service, THE LIBRARY OF CONGRESS."

. . . concerning the priority of claims of commission sales representatives in bankruptcy proceedings.
"Attention is invited to section 104 of title 11, United

States Code, which provides a priority with respect to wages and commissions not to exceed $600 and earned within 3 months of the commencement of the bankruptcy proceedings. There has been no change or modification of this priority subsequent to the publication of the 1970 edition of the United States Code." Reference is made to a couple of bills introduced in the House of Representatives ". . . still under informal consideration of the Committee on the Judiciary (which) propose, in addition to a complete revision of the statutory language, an increase of such protection or priority to $1,200.00."

Well—so—how do you handle the overdue commission situation? Of course, if you are sure of your relationship with the principal, that no one is going to fire you just because you ask for your money, nothing further need be said on that score—except *that*! Ask! Do it! There might just happen to be some inside problems *you* are not aware of that *could* eventually interfere with that friendly relationship! And in any event—you're not interested in having this principal use the money due you for purposes of his own—are you?

It *is* embarrassing to have to ask for money due you, when you know the other fellow knows it is due, but there are several approaches you can try before turning the matter over to your attorney. The one this writer always liked best, though not always feasible, was in one way or another to put the onus on a third party. I don't mean the bill collector. I'm speaking of being in a situation that has not yet reached the necessity for extremes, of cases where, instead of paying you *by the tenth of the month following shipment*—which is now pretty much standard timing for issuing commission checks—this principal happens to be two, three or, say, four months behind. Long overdue, a dangerous situation—but still retrievable.

A moment's digression; perhaps you have a principal who self-righteously proclaims as a matter of regular policy, that he doesn't pay commission until he gets paid by the customer for the order the rep turned in. If you have such a throwback to the nineteenth century in your roster of principals and you don't mind financing him (which is what you are doing in such a case) okay — but if you are that affluent, it is suggested that you try money lending as a regular business. It might conceivably be more profitable than repping!

Well, back to that third party approach. This is another instance of where your trade association could be very helpful. The association sets up a rule or makes an arrangement with a national credit bureau or even establishes a committee of its own members for the purpose of handling credit situations. Let the mere fact that such a thing exists be known. It might be well to publicize it in national trade publications (but check your choice of wording in such publishing with an attorney!)

Okay — now, for example, suppose you "just happen to mention" the existence of this to your delinquent principal. Perhaps you do it in the form of scribbling a little note — a very friendly warning — to your sales manager, telling him real confidentially this is embarrassing but that you are going to have to report this delinquency to your trade association's credit department according to your association's rules but that, of course, you'd rather not. Couldn't he drop a word in the bookkeeper's ear about the amount being overdue and to see that the check is sent out promptly? Thanks, old man — appreciate your help . . . etc., etc.

Now, suppose that tactful approach is too soft to do it. A little harder, perhaps, is to have in preparation for such problems a standard statement form of your own. You make it out as any account receivable department would in sending out monthly statements, showing the month in which the obligation to you was incurred, and the amount —

but *typed*. Then, *handwritten* across it in red ink a personal, "Please!" over your initials or first name.

Well, suppose that doesn't do it. You have to be tougher. The situation calls for strong action. In that event, you get right to the point — the showdown — and, always more effective than written "please remit" pleas: *talk* to your key man in person. *Afraid to ask for your money?* Weigh the facts — the actual risks involved in asking or the possibilities of losing the money you've earned and which is rightfully due you. Can you take a chance? That's up to you.

An excellent approach, if you still don't feel too hotted up about the situation, is a lightly worded note to your key man, *handwritten* by you rather than typed by your secretary, in order to indicate the personal confidentiality of the situation — in which you say, "It embarrasses me to have to ask for the money long due me, but it's even more embarrassing not to have the wherewithal to pay for my groceries (or my rent, or similar). Halp! !" Note that "embarrassment" is in itself always *the key word*.

Incidentally, a kind of reverse English situation often occurs when your principal asks you to collect from an account whose payment for an order *you* took is now overdue, and from a customer whose good will you'd hate to lose. Nevertheless, you are morally obligated to help out in such cases and, after all, if the customer doesn't pay up, your commissions are going to be charged back, no? And your principal is going to be very unhappy. So you drop that customer a note, something like this:

> *Dear (first name of Customer):*
>
> *It's embarrassing for me to ask that you take care of the (principal's name, invoice number, date, amount) but their credit manager insists that I contact you about it. I'm sure you've been busy and must have overlooked it so now won't you please forward your check immediately in order that we*

*can continue our pleasant relationship and be in a position to
serve you again as in the past?*

*On the other hand, if there is some special reason why this
account has not been paid, would you please let me know so
that I can take steps immediately to straighten it out?*

With best regards . . . . . etc.

At this point, let me interpose observance of a basic rule
in making collection efforts *regardless* of from whom the
money is due. That is, when your subject says vaguely, "I'll
take care of it" or even, "I'll take care of it next week" or "in a
few days" or "next month"—*don't stop at that. Pin him down to
a precise date.* That is a *must* for successful collecting—that a
definite date has been fixed as a reference point. If he
doesn't come through accordingly, you've got a strengthen-
ing of your position to say (or infer) accusingly that "You
promised payment on (name the date)." You've now got *two*
charges against him—the money he owes and his broken
promise. It puts him on the spot to pay up or else—much
more difficult for him to get from under without making the
required payment.

As I write about the subject of embarrassment in
asking for money due, comes back to me a strange, ludicrous lesson I learned many years go—in offering an
ironical commentary on unchanging human nature.

In the late 1920's I was a young radio retailer, operating a store on a busy Los Angeles street corner, a
common streetcar transfer point for downtown shop-
pers. At about any time of the day, one could see women
standing around, waiting for the streetcar. In those
days, business phones were billed on a five-cents-per-
local-call basis.

The upright phone standing on my desk was clearly
visible through the store's glass front, which led to
women frequently coming in and asking to use it. The

fact that they had to pass my radios on display, that I might thereby happen to attract a customer, seemed reason enough not to discourage this traffic. Besides, I was so very young, easily embarrassed, and it would have been difficult for me to refuse consent even though, at times, I was concerned when one of these people tied up my phone and thereby perhaps interfered with someone trying to reach me on a business matter.

Accustomed to all the services the department stores were educating women to expect, they had no hesitation in not only using my facilities, mine being a downtown business which gave it a kind of public connotation, but many of them failed to so much as say, Thank you. When the phone call was concluded, the woman would simply sweep out of the store, apparently her only concern now being not to miss her streetcar. *Not one* offered to pay the five cents her call was costing me which, in those pre-inflation years, was enough to buy me two doughnuts (half of a de luxe lunch for me, to accompany a cup of coffee for another nickel — when I wasn't brown-bagging it).

I left hinting signs around, pointing up that 5¢ per call charge. I placed a little box near the phone with a message lettered on it to read, "5¢ per phone call" — etc., etc. Nothing worked. One day a woman tied up the phone, making several gossipy-sounding kind of calls in a row, on a morning when I was anxiously awaiting a call from a prospective buyer of an expensive radio. That time, I lost my temper. I blocked her way and held out my hand demanding fifteen cents. In a great huff, she paid me, along with a stream of invective. Though she was at fault, I reflected why was I the one who had to be embarrassed? It gave me a new idea!

I typed a little sign on a bit of cardboard, cut an opening in it so that it would pass over the phone's mouthpiece, to be in a position so that the phone user's eyes couldn't possibly miss it. It read, "Every phone call costs us five cents—*including yours.* Please spare us the embarrassment of having to ask you for a nickel."

The results were like magic! I never missed, from there on out! Not once!It was astounding. Without a word from me, *not one person* from that moment on left without paying the five cents due! I even had to begin carrying substantial amounts of cash on hand to make change for the women who tendered payment of five cents with folding money!

I can only surmise that my little admonition must have been tied in with the depression syndrome of those years—somehow remindful of the common reference to people begging, selling apples for a nickel, ten cents a dance and all that! You must remember that a nickel was still useful money rather than practically nothing much more than a mathematical figure, as it is today. I have no explanation for it otherwise except that the experience taught me, as the profound words of some ancient philosopher once put it, people are funny.

At any rate: if it's money legitimately earned and due you and it's long and unreasonably overdue, *ask for it!*   ☐

28

THE REP EMPLOYER'S "ASSOCIATES"

On being the other fellow's boss

In addressing this chapter to heads of the more sizable independent rep firms, say from those employing several outside people to the larger, multi-manned rep organizations, it is naturally necessary to make due allowance for specific employment conditions varying from one industry to another — as for example, whether or not extensive technical knowledge is an important requirement. However, the principles involved in maintaining a productive, loyal staff of sales people, the methods of remuneration, establishment of ambients calculated to attract and keep good men and the philosophy of one's personal relations with employees, are subjects of concern entering into the operations of all sales agencies.

The hiring of new sales people is a whole other thing in itself, on which plenty of special books and lecture courses are available. For our purposes here, let's just first make a quick pass at where you start looking for desirable employees — then for some very plainspoken comments on your relationships with them after you've made them "associates."

From buyer to seller: I am reminded of the grousing comments made by a veteran rep friend of mine, with his disgusted, "Everybody you call on wants to go to work for you." In actual fact, the chances are that an excellent potential salesman really might be a buyer employed by a customer in your area. Such a man would start right in with

built-in empathy, knowing something of how the prospective customer thinks. By virtue of buyers' trade associations
and societies, their meeting and trade shows, no doubt he
has become a personal friend to many of those who may be
looked to as prospective customers for you. He will probably
know who's who in importance rating — a nice advantage to
have. Versed in the procurement end of his industry, he
might have some interesting trade figures in hand of
possible value.

Assuming he has the earmarks of making a good salesman,
you don't just crudely hire away such a person from your
customer's employ. The repercussions might not be pleasant
and there is such a thing as ethics! But assuming your
timing needs are not too urgent, you certainly have a right
to let be freely known, to sigh (out loud) as you make your
calls about how hard you're working, that you are short-
handed, looking for sales help. Trade gossip among your
customers may then carry your needs back to one who is dis-
satisfied with the conditions of his present job, who perhaps
sees no future there and would like an opportunity to make
more of himself. Without covert action on your part, you
have made it possible for *him* to approach *you*, to *ask* for the
job . . . Don't make it too easy for him. Certainly, prospective customers won't! Let him try to sell you on himself — a
good test of how he would fare if he were out in the field
selling for you. Before giving your final decision, confidentially *check it out with your customer, his boss* — ask if he is willing to give this man a break, a chance to better himself.
There is very little doubt but that he will say, Sure, take
him — and you haven't made an enemy.

If you advertise, trade papers are a good possibility for
sales people rather than the local "help wanted" newspapers.
The latter produce time-wasting responses because so many
people don't understand what independent sales representation is all about (a rep of my acquaintance who tried adver-

tising in the local classified help wanted columns received, among a number of eccentric requests for interviews, a letter from a barber applicant who asked what he meant by "resume"!).

Turning your search over to a reputable employment agency could be very helpful, emphasizing that the rep business is not suitable for the union philosophy, nor for any whose questions revolve around vacation periods, hours they would be expected to work, old age pensions and so on. Not that these matters wouldn't be taken care of in your arrangements with your employees—of course they would—but, initially, you would want to narrow your search down to a man primarily looking for a chance to build a career for himself, one expecting to work by the job rather than the hour.

Now, let's assume that you have your staff filled out with people who realize the meat-and-potatoes of good selling is know-how and hard work.

I

I hope this won't strike you as too cynical but, as a burnt child living in a realistic world, I would point up that a Numero Uno mistake of the head man in a business organization is if he attempts to gain the cooperation of his sales people by social fraternization, by making of himself "one of the boys." In establishing such intimacy, he abrogates his authority, has to overlook carelessness and lack of sufficient attention to the less obvious needs of the business, invites a lackadaisical attitude when he presents plans calling for all hands to take part. Most of all, he loses respect for the fact that *he* is the one responsible for having built the company to major proportions, that it was *his* long hours, *his* hard work, *his* sacrifices, *his* sweat that built the enterprise which provides the jobs for them.

A ship without a respected captain invites disaster. Someone always has to be in control. You're the man in charge; let the fact be known. In their most natural aspects, the respective differences in philosophies make separate entities of management and employees although, of course, the distance between them should never be insurmountable.

That doesn't mean you should revert to the anachronistic, whip-cracking type of boss. Forget it! A good salesman won't take it—he doesn't have to. There is no place for robots in the occupation of manufacturers' representation, for mind-deadening, autocratic treatment of employees. When Napoleon instituted the now-famed Legion of Honor in 1802, with membership granted for distinguished civil or military merit, he is quoted as having said, "Pin a blue ribbon in a man's lapel and he'll give you his life." We have outlived the implied cynicism of that comment; nevertheless, he was describing that trait of human nature—all-important ego, if you will—which makes recognition of achievement so important to a man. In the case of your "associate," that recognition is a meaningful part of his remuneration.

But in general—be *the general! Be soft spoken, be tactful, but let it be known who's in charge. In the long run you and your "associates" will be the better for it.*

II

The most important ingredient for attracting and holding good sales people depends of course on what you supply in the way of *incentive*. The main drawing card may not be the salesperson's *base* pay, whether salary, drawing accounts, guarantee, etc. No doubt you will have provided medical insurance and, with its manifest advantages nowadays, you probably have adopted a good pension plan, perhaps also a year's-end profit-sharing deal along with various other assorted goodies like paid vacations, holiday pay and so on. And, one can't say too much for recognition of achievement. But—over and above all— a most highly desirable feature of your salesman's remuneration could very well be *a monthly commission check*, regardless of what else he gets!

Keep in mind that the best salesman is the one afire with ambition, eagerly working hard, a man who passed up straight salary jobs that meant working for some large corporation as a nonentity—in short, a man like yourself (you should be so lucky!). Think of how *you* look forward to the commission check and consider how he, too, if it's big, will delightedly do his utmost to repeat and better it the following month or, if it is disappointingly small, will be prodded into working still harder in order that the next month's check be bigger.

That prospective commission check practically within vision at all times, is the dangling carrot we all need for keeping us on our toes, fighting for it . . . The monthly commission check procedure should be a primary feature of whatever your financial remuneration plan might be.

And further: I would make the periodical compensation in the form of *two* checks—the first, his base pay and the second, the commission (*incentive*) check. That would mean he would be bringing home like a monthly "bonus," which he might set aside, earmarked in a special account for perhaps building a down payment to buy a house, to educate his children, a luxury vacation, and so on.

The cash do-re-me every month philosophy means more than *things* and beats long waits like the year's-end for his accolades. A trip to Hawaii may be all very well but perhaps he'd rather take his wife and go on a mountain packing trip when *they* are ready for it. A new style digital watch is very nice but he already has a serviceable watch—he'd rather have the money towards a car for his wife. And so on. There's an element of psychology there—*whatever* may be the reward as an incentive, the best bet is he'd rather have it in *cash*, to buy whatever *he* pleases with it. You're dealing with human nature!

III

A good salesman doesn't take the orders; he persuades the buyer to give it. You may have a salesman so full of vigor, so hard-working, achieving such outstanding recognition and favor with the customers that you may have to make a decision about retaining him in your employ because you now have to contend with the "star salesman" syndrome. That can be very bad or it can be just fine.

Study this high-powered salesman of yours. When he meets your principals, does he noticeably use the pronoun "I" rather than "we"? Does he brag of the firm's accomplishments or does he dwell on what he did to achieve an increase in sales volume? If his functions include carrying on correspondence with the principals, writing reports, requesting information and so on, does he sign the letters with his name under the firm's company name or does he sign with his signature first, perhaps not even including the company name?

If you have a factory visitor in town and you delegate your "star" to taking him around to visit customers, are you ever greeted the next day with the explanation that they unexpectedly wound up very late after the last call and so he had the visitor come up to his home, to "meet the wife," and does this seem to become something of a regular practice? Do you find frequent factory visitors seeming to take it as a matter of course that in calling on customers, it will be this "star" who will be their guide, rather than you or one of the other men?

Okay—by now, you probably understand what I am getting at. Now, I do not decry the man who simply overdoes it when speaking in terms of himself rather than using the collective noun "we" and other similar peccadilloes. What the hell—if a man's ego is a little over-expanded, so what—just so long as he *is* justified in bragging about his accomplishments. Not only that but, in fact, if he *is* good, I would cultivate him with a far-ranging eye looking to the future. I would think in terms of perhaps helping this man build up a percentage of ownership in the firm so that, comes the time when you want to retire, you have a ready, built-in buyer for your business.

But—if you deduce signs of that man making undue attempts to ingratiate himself personally with people from your factory, of treating them beyond the call of duty (such as the apparently unplanned evening at his home) watch it! If *you* had told this "star" to take your visitor out for an entertaining evening, to a show, or to the fights or whatever, at company expense, that's not what I'm talking about (although even so, it would be *so* much better if you yourself were the entertainment committee). A writer—at this distance—can't decide for you whether or not a "star salesman" is simply practicing good selling, or is making it his aim to gain favor with factory visitors to eventually leave you, taking those factories and visitors with him! It's up to you to be vigilant, en garde when it comes to forestalling *unnecessary* personal relationships between the "star" and your factory visitors while, at the same time, you have to aim at impressing your principals with the high caliber of your sales people. Yes, it's a tight rope to walk, but it comes with the territory!

Your principals have every right and should be encouraged to know these men who, regardless of their employee status, walk in on the trade and importantly present themselves as representatives of said principals. The relationship between your sales people and your principals should be friendly, of course, but if you insist on it being kept on a *formal* basis, you will keep the salesmen and the lines!

IV

Make your financial remuneration methods simple enough so that your salespeople can easily approximate what their earnings may come to. Avoid complicated formulas. A man has to budget, to plan, to dream . . . .

V

Set up objectives, goals, quotas, both long range and in immediate sight. Keep stimulating and feeding the spirit of competition.

Recognize achievement with special remuneration for extra-curricular results. Reward the man who uses his imagination, who is creative in thinking up ways to go after new business. Outstanding results may be greeted with a laudatory plaque, good as far as they go, or a verbal pat on the back—but such things are simply froth on the beer when compared to evidences of your appreciation created by handing him a special check for what he did!

VI

Your plans for remuneration should be flexible enough to meet with changing conditions, particularly if you are in an industry whose sales volume is apt to fluctuate from season to season or year to year. It should be geared to volume in a way that will assure the salespeople of benefiting by good business just as you might expect them to accept the consequences of bad periods. But—in any event—*security* is going to be uppermost in the salesman's mind. If you don't make it possible for him to be assured of a reasonably stable income, to put it bluntly, what does he need you for?

Which means, you don't drive a penny-wise bargain with a productive salesman if you expect to keep him. Share generously with him because, aside from flights of social consciousness, with "share the wealth" philosophies and all that, it's *just* **good business** *to do well by your "associates."*   □

29

DISTRIBUTOR EMPLOYEE SALES MEETINGS

and referrals

You're a rep who sells primarily to and through distributors. You've managed to get your line "in" with a major distributor whom you long wanted to "get." His initial order was a good one. Now, how about the repeat orders? Will you be getting them and how big will they be?

Well—that very much depends. That your line includes good, salable products, is not enough. Your job continues after the distributor has started stocking the line. You're going to have to render "service," but for real if you want your line to be considered a main line rather than a sideline with this customer.

That distributor is probably stocking a multiplicity of product lines, some of them no doubt competitive with yours. One of his most fundamental duties has to do with inventory control. What's going to encourage him to continue stocking your line in full, in sizable quantities? He's in a complex business, probably doing well to enjoy four or five turnovers per year. To achieve a 4 to 5 percent net profit, what will you do to help him reach that status, that will make him value your line above those others?

How about the sales people who wait on your distributor's trade? Aren't *they* the people who, in the final analysis, sell your products or *don't*—as the case may be? Isn't it tremendously important that you cultivate these people, get their friendship, show them how best to sell your line by stressing the key points, citing case histories, selling strategies, how to cater to the peculiarities of some kinds of customers?

Certainly, a most important assistance you can give your distributor is to educate his people to the selling features of your line. It follows that you will be holding sales meetings for his sales people, including his outside men and his phone and counter sales people. It is hard to conceive of an on-the-ball distributor rep who doesn't carry out this all-important function of properly promoting his lines. If he neglects this part of his job, you can pretty well make up your mind that the first order he gets from that distributor will be just about the last one of any real size coming up.

For those who may be new to holding educational sales meetings for the distributor's people, the techniques of putting these promotions on for presenting one's line are quite simple:

Naturally you first make practical arrangements with the distributor's management for when and where best to hold the sessions. Date it far enough ahead so that you can fully prepare for it and at an hour when you can be reasonably sure of getting good attendance and attention. You offer to pay for the coffee, but also you bring soft drinks, doughnuts and the like. You appear with full batches for all to be present of up-to-date catalogs, price lists and other such applicable material, along with sample demonstrators. If the items are small and not too expensive, provide samples for each person attending. If you ordinarily pass out giveaways (key rings, pens, calendars, etc.) this is an excellent time and place to do it.

Don't be fanciful with your talk; this is no time for oratory. Don't drag it out. Outside of perhaps a short joke or humorous sally here or there to help everyone relax, make it brief, pungent, informal and right to the point. If you have a factory man in town, your distributor customer will probably be even more cooperative than usual in agreeing to hold a special meeting for this authoritarian to address his employees, the thinking being that they will get good information straight from the horse's mouth.

Just be sure that your so-called expert on the line is not only articulate but that he isn't one who is likely to act like the other end of the aforesaid horse. A good speaker for the factory's products can be very helpful in pointing up salient, salable features, planting these points in the heads of all present, in turn for them to pass on. But many a rep has had months and sometimes years of hard work spoiled by some jerk whose purpose in coming out for a visit was for his personal enjoyment rather than taking seriously the task of meeting those who, according to his reckoning, weren't very important in the scheme of things. Sooner or later, every rep has to contend with one of these good-time-Charlies. Their lack of real interest, their insincerity, soon shows up. They do more damage than good. It goes without saying that you make every effort to keep the play-boys away from your customers.

Plan for and get permission to take enough time for the meeting that will allow for a question/answer period. Being employees, some of them may be diffident. Be informal. Call them out individually by name. Urge them to talk up—tell them that's what you are there for, to rap with them. Pass out business cards to each present, asking them to be sure to call you if they have any problems with your lines—that no one expects them to be experts on everything—that's what you're being paid for, you say.

Make a point of establishing their friendship. Those souvenir giveaways—hand the items out to each one individually *yourself.* Don't just leave a quantity with the head man to give out—*you* be the hero.

If previously agreed to by the management, put on contests strictly for the sales people, with attractive prizes for the ones who sell the largest volume of your line over a given period of time. (Be sure the prizes hold real value; otherwise the salesmen are apt to sneer among themselves, with a detrimental lessening of their sales efforts. If you can't afford good prizes, forget the whole thing. Some people use various forms of meritorious certificates, plaques and so on. Wall decorations have their places, but let's face it — there are more places to put cash. Material things count highly with those working for ordinary pay.)

Avoid scheduling the meetings at a time when sales people will be anxious to get away. Cultivate the sales people individually. Single them out for warm greetings as you pass through the distributor's premises. Call them by first name and encourage them to likewise address you. Build up their sense of importance because, my friend, they *are* all important to you!

REFERRALS

It is common enough for a prospective customer to seek out the representative of a manufacturer who makes the product in which he is interested. In turn, if it is the kind of item a distributor stocks, the rep naturally refers the prospect to that distributor. Unfortunately, there are situations when the rep's complacent feeling of satisfaction with himself for doing the distributor a good deed, would be rudely disrupted if he were to learn that, as often happens, the prospective customer wound up buying a competitor's product. Why? How forestall this sad outcome?

The usual reason when this happens is that the distributor was out of stock on that item when the prospect called. Not wanting to lose the sale, the salesman substituted another brand of a kind he did have in stock. Or, it could be, for one reason or another, the salesman waiting on the prospect pushed the merits of a competitive make, deprecating the brand which was originally specified in the enquiry.

Some reps take this lying down. They rationalize: well, you can't blame the guy for not wanting to lose the sale. Or—he doesn't like my brand—well, you can't please everybody. Etc. So, he shrugs it off.

Bull—*bleep! Must* you be a sucker? So much depends on whether or not your line is well regarded by the distributor. If it's an important line to him, you are in a favorable position to act. If so:

Let's go back to the moment when the person first called you with an enquiry about one of your products. Upon providing the necessary information, get his name and phone number. A couple of days later, phone him. Ask if he got what he enquired about and how he was handled by the salesman. (Fringe benefit: so far as this customer is concerned, you're making a good impression by your service and showing of interest.)

Now—if everything went as you intended, fine. If the customer got the item you referenced, and was pleased with the service, at a later date, *make sure to tell that to your distributor and the cognizant salesperson.* That accomplishes several things: one, you've given them a compliment—which in itself engenders good feeling toward you—no one ever gets enough compliments in this world. Secondly, while making points for yourself, you're issuing a subtle warning that you are policing your line, that if a referral you make isn't carried out as you intended, *you* are going to know about it.

Suppose they *did* sell your prospect a competitors' brand. You've learned that. Well—first, take it easy. Don't do anything if it happens only once. However—more than that is for the birds! And let your distributor know it! Make it plain that (a) he ought to be carrying more quantities of that item and (b) you want to cooperate with him by passing these referrals on to him but if he is going to give you competition, you may as well give the referrals on to *his* competition. Why not—can he blame you?☐

30

CHART OF ACCOUNTS,
BOOKKEEPING AND IRS

How to cut down on your need for aspirin

Among the necessary evils of existence as a manufacturers' representative are the variety of procedures for maintaining proper financial record for your internal requirements and to keep the Internal Revenue Service satisfied. One thing is sure: the period when a man could do his own bookkeeping in a notebook bought at Woolworth's was all very well when you could buy a cup of coffee for a nickel (assuming you had the nickel), back there when an automobile was priced in the same number of hundreds they quote today in thousands, and a five-cent glass of beer at the bar of your favorite saloon was accompanied by a help-yourself free lunch such as you couldn't buy today with a five-dollar bill.

Which takes us out of dreaming and drooling about antediluvian days and brings us up to the Standard Chart of Accounts designed some time ago and now revised by Mel Daskal, CPA, the well-known accountant whose witty but solid tips on financial subjects often appear in sales agency publications. Many members of the Manufacturers' Agents National Association and the Electronic Representatives Association have adopted this uniform method of keeping accounts; its usage has become widespread to good advantage. Aside from its obvious internal use advantages, not the least of its benefits is the means it creates for mutual interchange of industry-wide figures among the firms active in an industry. For example, for many years ERA has been making an annual national Financial Survey, gathering and presenting average figures for every operation in the course of carrying on a rep business. Individual firms are enabled to cross-check national averages with their own figures and conditions, to show up where they may be out of line or in proper step with their contemporaries, as the case might be. And now that it is possible to have computer service at very low cost, with all the tremendous advantages that offers in the way of speed and coverage of every phase of your business' finances, the chart assumes even greater value.

Because of its flexibility, the chart can be readily adopted by independent manufacturers' representatives whether your agency is a one-man or multi-operation. Used in conjunction with national average figures, it is not only a personal business management tool but also offers a setting out of your expenses for the IRS should you have to be audited. In negotiating with principals, it can be used to justify your true costs of doing business. It is the use of such a system that marks the difference between the run-of-the-mill rep and the professional.

In the pages to follow, you will find the chart reproduced with explanations of the computer bookkeeping and other ways in which it can be expanded, including a minimum chart of expense accounts for the one-man operation, as reprinted (with permission) from Mr. Daskal's article in "Agency Sales," the monthly magazine published by the Manufacturers' Agents National Association. Following that is an excellent example of a weekly salesman's "Expense Report" which he also prepared, as supplied by the Electronic Representatives Association.

A STANDARD CHART OF ACCOUNTS
DESIGNED FOR MANUFACTURERS' AGENTS

*If you stop and think about it, the one absolute require-
ment for information gathering for all manufacturers' agents
is a uniform chart of accounts. So let's begin with the area of
most interest—the expenses. Ignore the numbers in front of
each account, and I'll explain them later on.*

Chart of Expense Accounts
(Alphabetical)

5410. Advertising
5610. Amortization—leasehold improvements
5210. Automobile expenses
5220. Automobile leasing
5230. Automobile repairs and maintenance
5240. Automobile mileage allowances
5250. Automobile insurance
5260. Automobile depreciation
5420. Bad debts
5110. Business gifts
5430. Catalogs and literature
5050. Commissions
6010. Computer service bureau
6020. Computer supplies and expenses
6030. Computer leasing
6040 Contributions
5120. Customer expenses
6050. Depreciation—office furniture and equipment
6060. Dues and subscriptions
6070. Employee benefits
6080. Equipment leasing
5440. Freight and delivery
5310. Hotels, meals and tips
5810. Insurance—general
5820. Insurance—group
5830. Insurance—officers' life
6090. Interest
5710. Licenses
6100. Office supplies and expenses
6110. Outside services
6120. Parking

6130. Personnel selection
5320. Plane and train fares
6140. Postage
6150. Photocopy supplies and expenses
6160. Professional fees
5130. Reimbursed expenses—salesmen
5620. Rent
5910. Retirement plans—contributions
5920. Retirement plans—administration fees
5010. Salaries—officers/owner's draw
5020. Salaries—office
5030. Salaries—salesmen
5040. Salaries—warehouse
5450. Sales meetings
5460. Samples
5140. Selling and promotion
5470. Seminars and conferences
5060. Taxes—payroll
5720. Taxes—state income
5730. Taxes—property
5740. Taxes—others
5330. Taxicabs and car rentals
5510. Telephone and teletype
5480. Trade shows
5630. Utilities
5490. Warehouse supplies and expenses
5150. Xmas expenses

There you have it. There is not one expense which cannot be fit into one of those accounts. The purpose of the alphabetical list is, of course, for easy location of the needed expense titles.

For the One-Man Agency

First we'll go to a minimum chart of expense accounts for the one-man agency. Then we can pull it all together. These minimum categories are also the master categories for the large chart of expense accounts.

5000. Salaries and commissions
5100. Selling expenses

5200. Automobile expenses
5300. Travel
5400. Sales aids and meetings
5500. Telephone
5600. Rent
5700. Taxes
5800. Insurance
5900. Retirement plans
6000-6100. Administrative expenses

Chart of Expense Accounts
(by Category)

Now watch how the categories bring those account numbers into agreement. This is the way your profit and loss statement can be arranged.

5000. SALARIES AND COMMISSIONS
5010. Salaries—officers/owner's draw
5020. Salaries—office
5030. Salaries—salesmen
5040. Salaries—warehouse
5050. Commissions
5060. Taxes—payroll

5100. SELLING EXPENSES
5110. Business gifts
5120. Customer expenses
5130. Reimbursed expenses—salesmen
5140. Selling and promotion
5150. Xmas expenses

5200. AUTOMOBILE EXPENSES
5210. Automobile expenses
5220. Automobile leasing
5230. Automobile repairs and maintenance
5240. Automobile mileage allowances
5250. Automobile insurance
5260. Automobile depreciation

5300. TRAVEL
5310. Hotels, meals and tips

5230. Plane and train fares
5330. Taxicabs and car rentals

5400. SALES AIDS AND MEETINGS
5410. Advertising
5420. Bad debts
5430. Catalogs and literature
5440. Freight and delivery
5450. Sales meetings
5460. Samples
5470. Seminars and conferences
5480. Trade shows
5490. Warehouse supplies and expenses

5500. TELEPHONE
5510. Telephone and teletype

5600. RENT
5610. Amortization-leasehold improvements
5620. Rent
5630. Utilities

5700. TAXES
5710. Licenses
5720. Taxes—state income
5730. Taxes—property
5740. Taxes—others

5800. INSURANCE
5810. Insurance—general
5820. Insurance—group
5830. Insurance—officers' life

5900. RETIREMENT PLANS
5910. Retirement plans—contributions
5920. Retirement plans—administration fees

6000-6100. ADMINISTRATIVE EXPENSES
6010. Computer service bureau
6020. Computer supplies and expenses
6030. Computer leasing
6040. Contributions
6050. Depreciation—office furniture and equipment

6060. Dues and subscriptions
6070. Employee benefits
6080. Equipment leasing
6090. Interest
6100. Office supplies and expenses
6110. Outside services
6120. Parking
6130. Personnel selection
6140. Postage
6150. Photocopy supplies and expenses
6160. Professional fees

EXPANDING THE CHART

For those really big firms or owners who insist on even more detail . . . notice that we have already expanded the chart from the minimum categories having accounts ending in "00" to the preceding chart where all accounts end in "0." That last zero is for your use in obtaining further detail.

Example
Let's take account #5030: Salaries—salesmen. If you want a separate account for each man, you can use #5031 for the first man, #5032 for the second man, etc. Of, if you want branch office accounting, you can use #5031 for the first branch, #5032 for the second branch, etc. In other words, use the last digit for whatever further analyses you want.

If you want to break down the eleven *major* categories (#5000, #5100, etc.) further, you can use #5001 for salaries of the first branch office, #5002 for the second, etc. Finally, you can expand the chart by using the next *unassigned* number in the category. If you want another classification of selling expenses, add #5160 and next #5170. All those numbers are available for "other" expense titles. Your expanded chart might then look something like this (ask your accountant for help in this area):

5101. SELLING EXPENSES—BRANCH #1
   5111. Business gifts
   5121. Customer expenses

5102. SELLING EXPENSES—Branch #2
    5112. Business gifts
    5122. Customer expenses

Statistical Survey of Manufacturers' Agents

The use of this standard chart of accounts can benefit you in more ways than just your personal accounting needs. MANA can gather broad statistical information *anonymously*, but with uniformity—to provide for you an in-depth study of the averages so that you may compare your agency performance with that of similar agencies. Here are some examples of the comparisons you can make:

1) *Each expense category as a percentage of commission income.*
2) *Each sub-expense as a percentage of the category and[or commission income.*
3) *Statistics by industry represented.*
4) *Commission income as a percentage of sales.*
5) *Statistics by geographic area.*
6) *Number of people, square feet occupied, time zone, number of doors on the car you drive, age and attractiveness of your secretary, whether you take her to conventions, what your wife thinks about that, etc.*
7) *Commissions per salesman.*
8) *Per salesman—sales, expenses, profit, per call cost, age, average compensation, size of car he drives.*
9) *Owners' compensation and net profits.*
10) *Number of principals represented.*
11) *Details of principal contracts.*

I have not gone as far afield as you think. A few qustions added to the expense survey can produce all of the information above.

INTERNAL REVENUE SERVICE

The IRS does not understand manufacturers' agents! They see all that "travel and entertainment" and come running! A large enough statistical sample of manufacturers' agent expenses could be used to show the IRS our typical "averages." Your accountants could produce copies at the time you were audited. While averages do not justify individual expense deductions, they certainly help set the "tone" of the audit—when you are trying to explain why your "entertainment" deduction is twice the salary of the IRS man!

MORE CHART OF ACCOUNTS

Up to now we have discussed only the chart of expense accounts. To round out the package and to provide for statistical surveys of assets, liabilities, etc., here is the rest. (Now you can see why the expenses started in the 5,000's. Here are the 1,000's through the 4,000's.)

1000. ASSETS
1100. Cash
1200. Accounts receivable—trade
1300. Other receivables
1400. Inventory
1500. Prepaid expenses
1600. Prepaid taxes
1700. Property and equipment
1800. Accumulated depreciation
1900. Other assets

2000. LIABILITIES
2100. Accounts payable
2200. Accrued expenses
2300. Loans payable
2400. Taxes payable, other than income
2500. Income taxes payable
2600. Other liabilities
2700. Long-term debt

3000. CAPITAL
3100. Capital stock/owner's capital
3200. Retained earnings
3300. Paid-in capital
3400. Other capital
3500. Treasury stock

4000. INCOME
4100. Commissions
4200. Merchandise sales
4300. Less: Cost of sales
4400. Expense reimbursements
4600. Interest
4700. Warehouse fees
4800. Other

That completes the chart of accounts. You can expand these account titles and numbers in a similar manner to the detailed explanation about expense accounts. Again, we can survey in these areas and tell you some interesting things:

1) *The average assets of an agency in dollars — or as related to the size of the firm's sales.*
2) *The average bank balance.*
3) *The average liabilities*
4) *The average net worth*
5) *How much of the net profit the owner "leaves in."*
6) *Every kind of income analysis.*

COMPUTER BOOKKEEPING

The standard chart of accounts can serve another function in your daily operations. There are computer bookkeeping services available now for as little as $10 a month. The ones we use have their own computer and offer a flexible and non-technical service to the public.

The computer is extremely stupid — as we all know from trying to get our credit card and department store accounts rectified! The computer cannot read the alphabet. It only understands *numbers.* So, if we give it a number that *stands* for a word, it can be instructed to print out that word. You have been provided with an entire standard accounting system with a *number* for every account title.

Getting Started

To start the service, we give them our chart of accounts. Now they can instruct the computer as to what each account number really means (the "alpha"). Along with these "rules" we send the computer service the opening balances in each account. (We recommend that your accountant or bookkeeper oversees this transition.) You need only list this information on a sheet of paper. The people at the computer center will do the rest (keypunching). We now have our beginning "general ledger" in the computer.

Monthly Transactions

We have to let the computer know what happened in our business each month. We wrote checks, we received money (hopefully), and we spent money (always). For each transaction, we want to tell the computer two numbers:

1) The dollar amount of the transaction.
2) The chart of accounts number.

That's all! The information can be sent in various forms: a copy of each check you write (stub or voucher check—with account number), or a listing of transactions, or journal totals (ask your accountant). Even the adjusting of entries is simply a hand written task. You can correct for errors, adjust depreciation, ending inventory, etc. As long as you send in *account number* and *dollar amount.*

Here is an example of how to list your transactions (notice that the computer wants *numbers!*):

Account #	Amount
5410.	$102.10
5220.	212.00
etc.	

The Output

You can choose between a service that prints out considerable alphabetic detail and those (cheaper) that don't. Our office uses full "alpha" service and this is what comes

back:
1) A financial statement covering the current month and year to date, with percentages.
2) A monthly general ledger with the opening balances at the beginning of the period and the individual detail of every transaction for the month—with both names and amounts.
3) Cash disbursements journal, cash receipts journal, sales journal, purchases journal, general journal. (Check numbers are indicated in cash disbursements.)

Additionally
You can get them to add sales, commission, customer, salesman and line analyses! Extra bucks, but almost every big agency has something like this. The basic computer service charge is just $20 to $40 a month, and there are many such service bureaus. Your accountant should know of at least one.

HOW MANUFACTURERS AGENTS
SPEND THEIR COMMISSION DOLLARS

Here are Mel Daskal's current estimates of how manufacturers' agents spent their commission dollars in 1976:

Salaries (including owner)	62%
Selling and travel	8%
Automobile	6%
Telephone	4%
Rent and administrative	5%
Insurance	3%
Taxes	3%
Others	4%
	95%

EXPENSE REPORT   SALESMAN_____   WEEK ENDING_____ 19___

DAY	CITY & STATE	NO. CALLS	LODGING		OWN MEALS (TOTALS)			TRANSPORTATION AIR, RAIL, ETC.			LOCAL	AUTOMOBILE EXPENSE ❶ (ITEMIZE ON BACK)				ENTERTAINMENT ❷ (ITEMIZE ON BACK)			OTHER EXPENSES ❸ (ITEMIZE ON BACK)			DAILY TOTALS	
			CASH	CHGE.	CASH	CHGE.	CODE	CASH	CHGE.	CODE		MILEAGE	CASH	CHGE.	CODE	CASH	CHGE.	CODE	CASH	CHGE.	CODE	CASH	CHGE.
SUN																							
MON																							
TUE																							
WED																							
THU																							
FRI																							
SAT																							
TOTALS													@____ ¢ MI =									❺

IF FLAT MILEAGE ALLOWANCE PAID NO. OF MILES TO BE REIMBURSED _____ @ _____ ¢ MI = _____

TOTAL CALLS

EXPENSE COST PER CALL ANALYSIS ❻
(DIVIDE TOTAL EXPENSES, ITEM ❼ BY NO. OF CALLS)

E.C.P.C. $_____ EACH

NOTE: ABOVE FIGURE DOES NOT REFLECT TOTAL COST PER CALL WHICH MUST INCLUDE COMPENSATION AND OFFICE OVERHEAD

PREPARED BY _____

INSTRUCTIONS: WHERE CHARGES ARE MADE DIRECTLY TO THE EMPLOYER, OR ON AN EMPLOYER CREDIT CARD, ENTER IN CHGE. COLUMN, AND USE CODE BELOW. ENTERING APPROPRIATE LETTER IN CODE COLUMN. ALL CASH OUTLAYS, OR CHARGES ON SALESMAN'S CREDIT CARD SHOULD BE SHOWN IN CASH COLUMN.

C   DIRECT CHGE. TO EMPLOYER
D   DINERS CARD
E   AMERICAN EXPRESS
H   HILTON CARTE BLANCHE

A   AIR TRAVEL
R   RAIL TRAVEL
O   OIL CO. (SPECIFY)_____
X   (OTHER – SPECIFY)_____

COMPLETE REVERSE SIDE OF FIRST COPY AND FORWARD FIRST COPY TO YOUR EMPLOYER. RETAIN SECOND COPY FOR YOUR FILES. BE SURE TO COMPLETE ITEM ❻

❼ TOTAL AMOUNT DUE SALESMAN $_____

SALESMAN'S SIGNATURE _____

OFFICE USE ONLY ❼ TOTAL EXPENSE (TOTAL OF ❹ & ❺) $_____
APPROVED BY _____

REIMBURSED BY CHECK NO. _____
AMT. OF CHK. $_____   DATE _____

M. H. DASKAL, C.P.A.

NORTHWAY INDUSTRIES, INC., RT. 2, EAGLE RIVER, WISCONSIN

This form is especially designed to help you & your employer comply with the latest Internal Revenue Service rules regarding expense accounts.

You must itemize entertainment, automobile, and other expenses. (Columns marked ❶, ❷, and ❸ on the front of this form.)

If you receive mileage allowance, but want to keep a record of your own auto expenses for IRS purposes, do so on second copy only.

ANALYSIS OF ENTERTAINMENT, AUTO AND OTHER EXPENSES — — DETAILED ACCOUNTING OF TOTALS LISTED IN FRONT.

❶ AUTOMOBILE EXPENSES

DATE	AMOUNT	DESCRIPTION

❷ ENTERTAINMENT & GIFTS

DATE	AMOUNT	WHO WAS ENTERTAINED (OR GIVEN GIFT)	FROM WHAT COMPANY	PLACE ENTERTAINED (OR DESCRIPTION OF GIFT)	PURPOSE

❸ OTHER (TEL., TOLLS, ETC.)

DATE	AMOUNT	DESCRIPTION

NOTES:

31

THE VENDORS' EXHIBITIONS

Showcasing on the customer's premises

In the business world, the lone wolf has just about become an extinct species. Mankind's awareness of the need we have for each other, neuters the instincts of the predator. In our particular world of manufacturers' representation, sooner or later it becomes manifest that being united, as in the form of a trade association, is of benefit to each one as well as to all.

Vendors' Fair. The outstanding success of a continuing project developed initially by the Northern California Chapter of the Electronic Representatives Association a few years ago, has prompted similar groups across the country to engage in some like form of localized or regional suppliers' "Shows." The exhibition is described by the ERA chapter as its mini-show "Vendors' Fair." In brief: the suppliers' or vendors' exhibition consists of a limited size "Show," of displays by this organized group of manufacturers' representative firms in its own marketing area, set up for a few predetermined hours right on the premises of major manufacturing customers located in their territory.

Now established as a regular project of the membership, the Fair is also supplemented by an additional promotion described as the "Showcase Program." In this deal, specially constructed showcases are placed permanently on the customer's premises in strategically selected locations, particularly where personnel from the Engineering and Purchasing Departments habitually traverse. Participating association members, according to pre-arranged sequence, display their lines through scheduled one or two week periods, thus giving the customer's people a continually revolving "Show."

If your association isn't into such projects, the details following will tell you how it is done. If you don't *have* an association in your marketing category or haven't joined one that does exist in your area, the benefits from such mutual effort, in addition to all the other advantages of trade association activities, exemplify how important and rewarding cooperative programs can be.

The "Vendors' Fairs" are arranged for with customer management by a committee from the ERA, establishing time and place. The points made in soliciting appointments for putting the Fair on are that it is an efficient, time-conserving way, at no cost, for their procurement and engineering personnel to become familiar at one swoop with the "latest developments of the art," acquiring knowledge of the various products and the possibilities of using them without sales people taking up their working time.

From the exhibitor's standpoint: you're not confronted with trying to get the buyer's or engineer's attention when he may be occupied with other matters. He isn't made to feel he is a target. He looks around at exhibits leisurely, without any expectation of being pounced on by eager sales people. In most cases, the Fairs are held during the lunch period, when he is away from the interruptions of the phone or being harassed by any of the usual problems of the day. In short: you're presenting your picture to him when his mind is at ease, receptive and the education he is acquiring is under the aegis of management's approval.

The Fairs are usually spaced out some four to six weeks apart. Those members who take part display the newest of their products, aimed at drawing the interest of Engineering and Purchasing personnel. Rules are established and enforced, to make certain nothing occurs that would annoy the customer, and to assure being invited back again at some future time.

The individual member exhibitions are displayed on uniform folding tables, covered with a single color cloth, measuring 30 inches by 60 inches, or on a vertical enclosure of similar dimensions. The member may employ either but not both, and they must be light enough to be moved easily by one person. Card displays are limited to 20 inches by 24 inches maximum. No electric power is permitted because of the tangling of cords. Noise-making devices are strictly no-no.

Members are admonished to show products, not catalogs; literature for distribution must be kept under the table. The exhibitors are counseled to use imagination in creation of displays that stimulate the interest and prospective sales of the product shown, their sales talk to be low key. Preferred are products which tend to bring out late developments in "the state of the art" rather than the same old ho-hum products with which everyone is familiar.

Positioning of the tables is set out according to the committee's arrangement. Locations of the Fairs are variously in the customer's cafeteria, a courtyard, a parking lot adjoining the buildings or wherever may be worked out pragmatically with the management. Hours for the "Show" are usually limited to between 1 p.m. and 4 p.m.

Giveaway souvenirs are permitted, though not encouraged, but the exhibitors are asked not to make these too elaborate. Nothing is wanted that would detract from the *professionalism* of the Fair, that might be construed as of a circus ballyhoo nature. Handing out souvenirs is tolerated provided they be small and not expensive, such as the usual pens, pencils, rulers, U.S.-to-metric slides, charts, small notebooks, wallet-size calendars and so on. Attendants at the table are limited to two persons; one can be a member of the firm plus a factory man, if desired.

Inexpensive but colorful notices on 8½" by 11" sheets are printed individually for each Fair, according to where and when it is to be held. These are posted on bulletin boards, as well as distributed by the management and the reps throughout the plant a week or two in advance of the showing, also sometimes used to inspire publicity in local trade papers. To enhance interest among the customer's personnel and to be assured of good attendance, it is announced that a raffle will be held in which all attending will take part, the lucky winner's prize to be a calculator or a digital watch.

Members are admonished to remember they are guests within the facilities of the customer and to govern themselves accordingly. They must create no disturbance, cause no litter or any kind of possible irritation. If chairs etc. are moved about, they should be put back in their normal places at the Fair's ending. Members must observe the prescribed hours scrupulously, arrive and leave promptly at the times agreed, being sure to clean up thoroughly before departing from the premises.

The popularity and worth of this project cannot be overestimated. Members of the association have unequaled opportunity to talk with key engineers and buyers, as they stroll leisurely about, curiously inspecting the exhibits, asking questions. The reps deliberately refrain from bringing supplies of catalogs. In response to requests they explain, "No need for you to drag catalogs around — we'll mail them to you." That ploy gets them the visitor's name and proper address, his function with the company and a chance to size him up since he may very well be someone of importance whom they had not previously met, to make mental or written notes for future reference and for additional names to their mailing lists.

In Northern California, we found that managements were pleased enough with our "Vendors' Fairs" to ask for showing repeats each year. They like the fact that their personnel can inspect the vendors' offerings at leisure instead of being interrupted when they are busy, of taking up their working time, and they appreciate the opportunity of their people being educated to "what's new" without being subjected to sales pitches. The proof of the pudding is in the showings — such Fairs have been held, in some cases repeatedly, on the premises of some of the most famous manufacturing customers in the country, including GTE-Sylvania, Watkins-Johnson, Memorex, Hewlett-Packard, Philco-Ford, Lockheed, Varian, IBM, Singer and a number of others similarly famed.

THE SHOWCASE PROGRAM

The "Showcase Program" is a different promotion in that it consists of a showcase installed permanently in one or possibly two of the customer's buildings or departments, in carefully selected locations where the engineers and purchasing people pass frequently. At some of the larger manufacturing customers, two showcases might be set up — one in Engineering and the other in the Purchasing Department.

Basically, the program is a continually changing exhibit of (at least theoretically) new products, along with applicable literature — no attendants — nothing else — it's for viewing only. Each participating member is given an appointed period of time for displaying his lines — which may be limited to either one or two weeks, according to previous agreement. A schedule is set up for a year, with each member being assigned specific dates. Penalties are attached for failing to "show" as scheduled unless the member arranges for the substitution of another member taking the assigned period. *That week is the original assignee's responsibility.*

The display must never be empty; if a member fails to "show" twice when his turn is up, he is dropped from the schedule. The time of arrival and "clean out" departure have to be strictly observed. No samples, gimmicks or giveaways are allowed — only the products on display and the racks of literature. Members are asked to check once or twice a week to make sure racks are always filled.

The showing fixture itself is a case 36" long by 18" wide by

4 feet tall. It is covered by a removable acrylic plastic cover which is 12 inches high in the rear and slopes down to 4 inches high in the front, secured and removed by three screws on each side. Also a lock protecting the contents is installed to which members have keys.

Directly under the display area are nine compartments for literature to which viewers help themselves. Up to nine lines can be displayed providing they are small. The cost of the case will vary according to where it is made, of course, but in Northern California they have been costing the association $130.00 each.

The way this promotion is handled: good judgment has to be used in selecting the one or two members likely to know well or have access to the customer's key individual who is in a position to authorize the permanent placement of the showcase in the desired location, where it will always be in clear view. In other words, as may be understood, the success of the deal lies with the persuasive ability of the selected members to "sell" customer management on the "silent show" installation. Along with its benefits, assurances are given and followed up that the cases will always be kept up in good shape—clean, orderly, the racks filled with plenty of literature, the timing and displays to present new, interesting products rather than things which are old hat. That the "Showcase Program" is attractive is evidenced by the fact that they have been installed at Ampex, Hewlett-Packard, GTE-Lenkurt and others similarly famous.   □

32

PAST, PRESENT AND WHO KNOWS?

The crystal ball, as the centuries turn

A septuagenarian still alive today has lived through one age of mankind and the beginning of another. Born at the century's turn, a man in his seventies would have seen the nineteenth century metamorphosis from a rural dependent, earthbound existence, into the mechanical, the electric and the electronic periods, followed by mankind's release from gravity into outer space. Once again, pioneering mankind reaches out from the mundane to make way through the stars enroute to the imagination staggering, all but certain contacts with other worlds, as the twenty-first century approaches.

Rollo May says in his "Courage To Create" that "we are living at a time when one age is dying and the new age is not yet born." He isn't with it yet! With our rocketing sorties into outer space the sperm and arrival at the moon having completed conception, our cameras focused like tourists snapping shots of the Grand Canyon, we are already taking close-ups of Mars. It would seem the life of that next age is already started.

But what of today, of that microcosm of the universe which makes up one's own present world?

Chances are, if you are an established rep, you intend to continue in that occupation for some time to come. "Some" time? Like how long is a piece of string?

What are the projections for your industry and your place in it? Do you know? What's it going to be like fifteen, ten or even five years from now? Are you anticipating, preparing for the changes sure to come? Will the industry exist — in its present form — or at all?

Sure?

No one can expect definitive answers to such questions. However, one thing *is* sure — there *will* be changes and they should be anticipated insofar as is possible. The wise rep will do something more than shrug his shoulders and mutter, "Who knows?" He will follow pragmatic procedures for keeping up with the trends — some simple and obvious, others that might require a bit of digging, studying the indications that may enable him to forecast conditions much more climatic and meaningful than whether or not it is going to rain tomorrow. He will always keep in mind that changes can be expected in the offing which might place his entire life career at stake or, on the other hand, perhaps offer an opportunity for making a great step forward in his life.

> *One may reverse the laser of hindsight*
> *and focus it on the future.*

It is a sad fact but well to keep in mind that in recent times, some of our biggest or more common industries, having long served past generations, have faded from our lives or are patently falling by the way. Remember when the height of achievement was to be president of a railroad? Not so very long ago, eh? How'd you like to be in the railroad business today? Remember when the ladies used to have faded clothes dyed — or do it at home themselves? Do they, still? Aren't they more apt to discard them, to buy clothing formed from chemicals — cheaper and probably more attractive? What's become of the adding machines, the ones with a crank that you had to yank for each entry — every office had one — now replaced by electrical and, in turn, by electronic calculators or computers? Men's garters, starched collars — anyone wearing those today? Seems like just yesterday, our fathers did! Eyeshields made of celluloid, to wear at work in an office? When did you last seen an ink blotter, that common adjunct of the now practically obsolete fountain pen everyone once carried — the storage kind that had to be continually filled with ink?

There are men still living who remember the metal statues of animals decorating the fronts of the more pretentious homes. When the temperature sank extremely low, someone was bound to say euphemistically, "Whee, it's cold enough to bring in the brass monkeys." (If you don't know what that means, ask your father — after all, this is no *Playboy*!) Don't be complacent because yours may be one of the more stable industries. Even though comparatively young, you should be able to think of numerous items recently commonplace but that are already gone, buried in commercial history. If you don't believe changes in some substantial form can wipe out familiar products sold all day long, that they couldn't occur in your industry, just recall the changes in transportation from the ubiquitous horse and buggy era to railroads, to automobiles, to aeroplanes faster than sound, with earth-planetary travel already in sight — all happening within memory of the generation still with us.

Not only to illustrate the point directly from life but, in passing, I'm going to interpose a bit of human interest having to do with the extraordinary career of a man noted for his shrewd business acumen who, nevertheless, fell short in one detail — a stubborn, misplaced faith and refusal to look ahead to the plainly visible future, and it broke him. (I'd rather not name him here other than to say I knew him as my uncle.)

His first business venture was in the 1890's. With my father, these two entrepreneurs operated an "academy" for teaching people how to ride bicycles. (Honest! I have a picture taken at the time to prove it!) They were ensconced in a great barn of a building that had once been the Chickering piano factory, located on the edge of a chasm in what was then the far outskirts of New York, probably now the Bronx.

The man was tremendously handsome—stalwart, shoulders squared back like those of a veteran general, six foot plus, with facial features that seemed to be hewn from granite. The "academy" proved too slow for his adventurous temperament and, in any event, was petering out. He took off, crossed the continent to settle down in San Francisco. When gold was discovered in Alaska in 1897, he joined the hundred thousand prospectors who made up the gold rush, endured untold suffering in the frozen wilderness, found no gold, struggled back to San Francisco in a two-hundred-mile trek on foot. The bitter strain of the experience changed his appearance beyond ready recognition; his trembling fingers could not form the letters to make his signature acceptable when he appeared at his bank to withdraw some money. It became necessary to round up friends to identify him.

He started a bicycle business, got into motorcycles and, at the turn of the century, had become extremely wealthy as one of the first automobile dealers in the country. Came April 18, 1906 and the San Francisco earthquake and fire. He had been spending the night in a Turkish bath. Crawling out of the building wreckage, he made his way through torn-up streets to his place of business at 1442 Market Street—correction, what had once been a place of business! For him, the devastation of the great cataclysm was complete. His entire stock of cars, then valued at $50,000, was flattened out, to lie leveled before him as just so much rubble. He was broke.

Within a few weeks, he became a wealthy man again. Transportation through the torn-up thoroughfares of the city was limited to getting about on foot. As soon as telegraphic communication became established, he shot out wires to Eastern sources and brought in trainloads of bicycles. "I put San Francisco back on wheels" he used to brag.

He had a new building constructed to house a bicycle and

motorcycle business which grew to be one of the biggest in the West. He induced my father to leave his own insurance and real estate business, to come to California and work as his manager. They opened a branch in Los Angeles, which Pop managed and built up to a thirty-five-employee operation.

In 1914, my uncle was offered the Buick agency for California and turned it down. Pop was beside himself but there was no arguing with the man—he stubbornly refused to have anything to do with automobiles. As we put it today, he had had it. He was going great now, the proud owner of a widely renowned business selling big quantities of bicycles and, for those who wanted them self-propelled, he had motorcycles which he sold in great numbers anywhere from the kid trade to police departments.

Well—a man named Henry Ford had started producing automobiles based on a new manufacturing principle. Making robot-like creatures of his employees, excused by paying them considerably more than the going labor rate, he introduced a manufacturing process to be known as mass production. He flooded the country with his tin Lizzies. By the early 1920s, you could buy a Model T Ford for the same cost as a well equipped motorcycle. The man who had put San Francisco on wheels was supplanted and outdone by the man who would put all of America on wheels. It was the beginning of a new era in the movements of mankind.

His business going down hill with no stopping it, Uncle closed the Los Angeles branch store. Pop was given a $300 check (his salary at the end had been the munificent sum of $75 a week) and was summarily fired. A year or two later, Uncle went out of business in San Francisco. *He had failed to see the future looming up right in front of his eyes.* He died broke.

New to calling on IBM, upon introducing myself to one of their most important senior engineers, he said, "Soon as you have something that is smaller or will enable us to do it faster, we're going to be interested." People are always looking to progress. Suppose you were to be hit because what you sell is no longer in demand. Somebody has produced something better or cheaper or more attractive or more efficient because, because . . . as you read these words, people all over the world are working on products *which will supplant and obsolete those you sell today.*

But in addition to generally publicized trends, to converting, to exchanging information with contemporaries at trade association meetings, to thoughtful attendance at your principal's trade meetings and other such general avenues of information, one simple, widely prevailing procedure exists which can and should be followed to anticipate as best possible changes or developments in your industry of a nature which could be unfavorable to you — or, by the same token, might be wonderfully opportunistic. So obvious, right in your mailbox, it is perhaps the most commonly neglected.

Somewhat immodestly, perhaps, I am fond of quoting a reviewer who said of my writing, "That guy has been there . . . His is not theoretical, but a seat-of-the-pants presentation." Well, I very much agree — and as indicated, I had to learn the hard way! But *you* who are having at it today, have advantages which didn't exist when I was fighting the Battle of the Buck. Today, many good and timely business books are available, applicable courses can be taken in person or by mail, seminars are held by trade associations and various business groups. To benefit from the extremely valuable experience presented by trade associations bearing on "the state of the art" in your industry, calls for no more than the cost of being a member. *But at your finger tips* are daily, weekly or monthly publications presenting pictures of what goes on in your industry, of what may be expected in the future — just a wealth of the most important, meaningful kind of information is yours for the taking, waiting to smooth out *your* way. As to that printed matter: let's look between the covers of trade publications and business journals.

It is unfortunate that because so many trade publications come for free, their publishers looking to advertising for their revenue, many people depreciate their worth—a characteristic of human nature, which is to assume things must be costly before considering them valuable. How many times I have heard reps perfunctorily dismiss their industry's trade papers or business journals of the day, admittedly passing up the reports and articles of good staff writers on the better publications along with their selected special guest authors.

Not that reading your industry's printing output is going to make you a big success, per se—although something or other you just happen to run across in one of its publications, *could* inspire you to do *something* you hadn't thought of that might just help you advance on the road to riches. No doubt, many who read this book are long established, experienced sales people, to whom some of the situations described herein are old hat. One might note, too, that reading a book of this kind is ideal for veterans to review much of what they once knew but had forgotten. BUT—and it's a big but—that portion which *is* new to them might very well pay in return thousands of times what this book costs! Then, too—by a process only God—and I do mean Him—can explain in the course of reading this or some other business book, trade magazine or newspaper, a mental relay snaps into contact, establishing a circuit from the printed page to the reader's eye, on through his brain—we call it inspiration or AN IDEA. Ask any successful business man if he hasn't had such an experience. You'll find he'll answer in the affirmative.

To employ hindsight and foresight at the same time would seem to require an extra pair of eyes in the back of

one's head or to induce a feeling of being somewhat schizophrenic. Nevertheless, to disdain industry studies and forecasts by authoritative figures is simply to hide one's head in
the sand.

> *There were these two girl ostriches strolling across the
> desert sands. One looked back and saw two boy ostriches fol-
> lowing. "Goodness me," she cried, "we must run!" So they
> did—but the boy ostriches kept gaining, had almost caught
> up.*
>
> *The other girl ostrich cried out, "Quick—we must hide!"
> They stopped and hid their heads in the sand. The boy
> ostriches came up, halted and looked about in all directions,
> puzzled. "I'd have sworn—" said one and the other agreed, "I
> just can't understand it. Where did they go?"*

Well, as human beings, we don't physically hide our
heads in the sand but in many cases the effect is the same.
What should be evident is this: in trade publications and
business journals, knowledgeable and articulate people, of
outstanding industry authority, give you the benefit of far-
reaching research which *you couldn't afford on your own*!
Ordinarily, you'd welcome an opportunity to *hear* a man
lecture who is looked up to and respected in your industry,
wouldn't you? What's wrong with *reading* what the same
man has to say in trade publications or business journals?
You have the benefit of their expertise before you, simply
for taking a little time to read what they have to say—for the
price of a magazine subscription (and sometimes not even
that!)

I recently read a special study of the manufacturers'
selling problems in all its various facets, in a special edition
of a well known sales and marketing publication. Among
the charts and various compilations, was a tremendous
amount of material to give any marketing/sales manager
pause for thought. It went into great depth on the subject of

modern marketing. That study in itself could have considerable significance, for example, in determining whether or not to switch from a staff of direct selling salespeople to the independent rep system. It could very well have been perused by the far-sighted professional for unprejudiced indications of trends in product distribution. A rep could find therein figures of considerable significance brought to bear on his present occupation, to say nothing of providing neutral but meaningful data to reinforce his contention that selling through independent sales agents could be at lower cost and more productive than through direct sales people.

That was only one lone example of priceless information easily available that could significantly influence one's future. What it boils down to is that trade publications try their utmost to keep up with current developments, to look ahead, to publish important articles by knowledgeable writers—men in a position to review and prognosticate, whose backgrounds make their forecasts authoritative. The editors rub elbows with leading figures in their respective industries, to pass along what they learn to their readers.

The ostrich hiding its head in the sand may lose out only on perhaps a pleasurable date, but the human being who fails to face up to the facts of life when they are set out before him in cold print, is missing potentialities that could affect his entire existence for better or worse. For the expending of a little time and a little effort the payoff can be mighty big! ☐

POTPOURRI

From the author's notebook

Watch the ego

When you're explaining something to your prospect — whatever it may be, such as the characteristics or construction of what you are selling — for heaven's sake, don't say, "You follow me?" Whenever I hear this example of thoughtless egotism, I'm tempted to respond with, "Yup — right behind you — in good position to give you a kick in the pants." Same goes for such as, "You understand?" or any similar deprecating words calculated to make your listener resent the implications — causing him to think his own question, such as, "Who the hell does he think he is? Does he consider me a dummy?"

The way to put it is, of course, "Am I making myself clear?"

*　　*　　*

To get on a first-name basis

It's obvious enough that to be on a first-name basis with your trade is desirable. But note this: your customer may be just as diffident when it comes to addressing you by *your* first name, as vice versa.

To get this intimacy started, when you phone him, or want the receptionist to announce you, use *your* first name with your surname when you're asked, "Who's calling?" When you talk with him directly, identify yourself by pronouncing your first name followed, if necessary, by your surname. That encourages him to pick that up, to address *you* by your first name — which you can then take as tacit approval to use *his* first name when you're addressing him and so, now, you're friends!

*　　*　　*

Extending the usefulness of a good camera

Unless you are making calls where carrying a camera is forbidden, you can sometimes use a camera to mighty good effect for business purposes:

1. Snapping a picture of the buyer at his desk, to later send him a copy with your compliments, will bring a pleased smile to his face! It's great for building good will (a subtle way of flattering him). There are several choices of cameras available nowadays small enough to be easily carried in your pocket, even those with a flash feature.

2. Sometimes a questionable product apparently giving trouble is too heavy or solidly installed — it cannot be readily returned to the manufacturer for inspection. To take a picture of it, may help in searching out the problem.

3. For some situations, a picture of a competitor's product or a set of conditions illustrating a prospect's problems, will help simplify what would otherwise involve lengthy, complex explanations.

4. Pictures of yourself and office staff are nice for holiday greeting cards or, if really good, to use as an enclosure when soliciting a line.

*   *   *

Line wanted

Here is a guideline for a somewhat "different" wording in advertising for lines:

REGIONAL SALES MANAGER
with skilled staff, now providing sales
representation (also mail promotion
and warehousing) for a select group of
manufacturers in (describe territory);
have opening for one more quality
line.* Write or phone
The ZYX Company
etc.

*Include classification of the kind of line you are seeking. Also insert "technically oriented," if applicable, or "consumer products," "for department store trade" etc. — whatever your specialty might be.

*   *   *

Get well quick

I've written about this before but it very much bears repeating. Having been the object on occasion of what I am suggesting, I can testify to its tremendous impact. If you know somebody who is ill, in the hospital, be sure to do something about it. Don't wait for the funeral — he can't smell the flowers! A "get well" card at least, or better, a handwritten note of cheer, a magazine, candy, flowers, a book, (especially nice is a plant he can take home with him to re-plant — it symbolizes renewed hope that all will be well) — unless you have been there, you just can't realize how tremendously meaningful these things are to the patient. But, further — if you will extend your attentions to the point of making a phone call enquiring about his progress or — the bestest of all! — go so far as to call on him in person. In such event you can order the correct size halo for yourself in advance because you unquestionably will be included among the angels when your time comes — the patient receiving such attention will have nominated you for that distinction in his prayers. Pending that last moment, you will have a friend for life.

*   *   *

A classy touch

A touch of distinction some use most effectively for letterhead: have an artist design a logo for an embossing seal, to read with your company name and a brief slogan or motto ("renowned for service," "service that counts," "founded in 1958" etc.). Print from it embossed, self-adhesive labels — not too big—hold to a maximum of an inch-and-a-half or so—to stick on your letterhead. Also, very small, ditto for making your calling card outstanding. Costs a few bucks but very impressive.

*   *   *

A different giveaway

I wrote once of the success and fun I had with a 3¢ pencil that I handed to the buyer with the pretended admonition that it was a "special pencil," manufactured only for writing orders, worthless for any other purpose. Here is another little whimsy which can be used with light spirit, a "different" item which the recipient is likely to keep before him and which has the not inconsiderable virtue of being inexpensive:

This is the common wire hinged clothes pin, either the well known wooden kind or the newer plastic versions. Have printed to the proper size self-adhesive labels to read with (a) your name and phone number and (b) others with the words EVENTUALLY or TOMORROW or URGENT or TOP SECRET or FILE or SOME DAY or any words particularly related to your activities. You stick one on one side of the clothes pin and your name and phone on the other. These you assemble in sets as a giveaway.

The usage is, of course, for the buyer to employ the pins on his desk as spring clips to classify and hold batches of papers conveniently, thereby to mean constant handling of the clip with your name and phone number always coming up before him.

I'm sure a variety of labels for them will occur to you, once you have them. For instance, you're hand delivering a catalog: have it held closed with one of your clips labeled, NEW. Ditto for a quotation—or new price list—with clip label reading "NEW" or "SPECIAL" and so on. Use your imagination for labels fitting to your business. The novelty of the clothespin clip is bound to get you unusual attention.

To make the clothes pins a bit more attractive if you use the wooden kind would be, before sticking the labels on, to dip the clothespins in paint, each a different color—perhaps one red, the second white, the third blue or, according to your own ideas in color schemes. (If you use a distinctive matching color for all your printed matter, make these the same color.)

Incidentally, preparing these clips as per above, would be a nice little project for your youngsters, if they are still small.

*   *   *

Titles

Except where formalities are mandatory, though you may be a one-man operation, avoid referring to yourself by that corny sounding "proprietor." It is too reminiscent of the ancient, cracker barrel, pot-bellied stove atmosphere. Promote yourself at least to "Manager." If, as and when incorporated you become "President," of course, and when you have one or more salesmen, employ resounding titles such as "Manager, Industrial Division" etc. By the same reckoning, your secretary becomes "Office Manager," perhaps "Administrative Assistant" (of course, if that means paying her a bigger salary, you may have to give this further consideration!).

You'll have to work up such glorifying job descriptions as may be fitting in your case—I'm only suggesting that you do it. I suppose counseling the adoption of chest-swelling titles may be considered cynical, but that's the way it is. People are like that. It's best to go along. I gave up trying to change people not long after leaving school—I found I was no competition for God—particularly upon learning that the French expression about things never changing certainly applied to human nature—it always remains the same and a businessman might just as well bend his efforts to conform with it—in this case to observe that people are impressed by

a uniform, a book's cover and a man's title. What the
hell — in many cases, the object of the decorative terminology may even live up to it!   ☐

TEN COMMANDMENTS FOR MANUFACTURERS' SALES REPRESENTATIVES

1. Don't grab a line because it happens to be available. A professional doesn't "pick up" a line "just to see if it's any good." Give that manufacturer full evaluation before you agree to become his representative.

2. Don't refuse to handle a line only because it is small. Look ahead—carefully consider its potentialities—otherwise when it becomes big, it's the other fellow who's likely to have it.

3. Don't miss attending the conventions in your industry. These get-togethers are for exhibitions of what is going on in your world, for meeting of the innovative, the thoughtful and the best minds in the industry. You should be there.

4. Don't overlook any possibilities for publicizing yourself. Many people who speak in glowing terms of a man's reputation, are often likely to have arrived at that state of adulation simply from seeing his name in print.

5. Don't knock the sales manager who terminates you. It does no good, it leads to wondering why you doth protest so much. Besides, he may turn up at some future time as sales manager of one of your choice lines.

6. Don't describe closely the equipment or the purchases of one of your customers to another. You might get the reputation of being a gossip, of one who carries the private affairs of one customer to another. The latter could even be an unknown competitor.

7. Don't get too close in cultivating the friendship of your customer's secretaries and receptionists.

8. Don't neglect to have your attorney check a new sales contract. These pieces of paper are steadily becoming more and more meaningful in independent manufacturers' representation.

9. Don't neglect to take out product liability insurance. The courts are apt to include the sales representative in the line of distribution.

10. Don't neglect your reading. Go back over the better books you have read. Extract key portions and write them out as they might conceivably apply to you; helps fix them in your mind. Upon re-reading a book, you might be surprised at how much you've forgotten that you once knew, of subjects which perhaps didn't mean much when you first read about them but suddenly loom up big in your life. □

ADDENDA

Dear Reader:

This book was intended to have been concluded with the preceding "Potpourri" notes and the "Commandments." As a separate project, I had in mind following at a later date with a story or essay, perhaps to be magazine published, its theme to stem from the mystique of business success. It would trace the highlights of a man's life from his first job to a climactic, crashing fall from the heights of a high-powered executive position, followed by his search as a fifty-year-old man for a job in a world groveling at the altar of youth. With statistics of psychologists telling us four out of five men are in the wrong job, it would bring out the fact that it is possible even under the most unlikely, adverse circumstances, for one to become the fifth man, thereby to enter into a bright new world.

Well, at the last minute, almost as the book was being readied to go to press, I decided to finish it up and include the story herein. Employing the guise of easy reading fiction, the intent is to introduce practices, ways and means for the reader to consider, perhaps to adopt, perhaps to find motivating ideas therein helpful for smoothing out the hard road to success.

So, sit back, relax, and read the story of Stann B. at your leisure, with my assurance, for whatever it may be worth, stemming from the successes I have witnessed in the course of a very long lifetime, that what others young and not so young have done, *still others can do*. Including *you*. Why not?

With all my good wishes,

Sincerely,

Frank deBell

ONLY IN AMERICA!

To lose the position he had assumed was to have been a lifetime career:
—at age fifty, to trudge job-seeking through a humiliating gamut of fast turndowns resulting from his birthdate looming up with neon-bright glare on the application forms;
—To see his bank account balance dwindling to a low three figure and his wife, long out of the job market, worriedly scanning office help wanted ads;
—the couple to bask lazily some years later in their deck chairs, enjoying a luxurious round-the-world cruise by way of celebrating his retirement from the occupation of manufacturers'representation —is one of those "only in America" stories of emergence from the struggles of making a living, out to lolling in golden age affluence, but which stems from real life. Call this one:

EVOLUTION OF A SALES REPRESENTATIVE

Fresh out of college with a degree in mechanical engineering, Stann B. (which will do as a handle for our purposes here) landed a job as a draftsman with a small hardware manufacturer. About a year later, the draft board was breathing down his neck and, as he put it, to avoid catching cold, he enlisted in the Army and was sent to training camp. He wasn't good at soldiering. Though no radical, the reactions of a free spirit to regimentation sometimes approached open rebellion. On one historic occasion, just before being readied to be shipped "over there," the dam gave way.

He had the barracks window washing detail that morning. While squirting a hose across the glass, his other hand holding the squeegee, the morning's skies made good their threat and let loose with a heavy downpour that soon soaked him through and through. Running for cover, he bumped into his sergeant. To his amazement, the sergeant ordered him back to the window washing job.

"But it's raining," Stann protested.

"Sir!" admonished the sergeant.

"Okay—sir—but it's raining like hell—sir!"

"You got your order, soldier! Get with it!"

"Are you nuts?" Stann could not contain himself. "In the rain? Why?"

The sergeant poked an emphasizing finger into the rebellious GI's chest. Instinctively, Stann grabbed at it, to push the fellow away. The other swung and landed. Enraged, Stann punched back. A furious fight started. Though soon separated by others, the sergeant lost a tooth and Stann's face was badly battered, the swelling not to go down for weeks.

He was saved from court martial by the fact that the doctor patching up the erstwhile antagonists, was himself new to Army eccentricities and secretly felt Stann had been justified in protesting the senseless order. He gave the men a stern lecture, with sarcastic admonitions about saving their fighting strength for the Huns. But taking the sergeant aside, he persuaded the glowering non-com officer to refrain from charging Stann with striking a superior by threatening he would take it upon himself personally to report him for issuing such a stupid order under the specious guise of discipline. He wrote up his reports as two separate "accidents" for their medical histories.

The incident was one of several foretelling the future when Stann was going to have to admonish himself that one salutes the uniform—not the man wearing it—but for one of his temperament, it was a philosophy he would find difficult to live with.

Stann served with distinction, he made captain, and had well recovered from shrapnel wounds by the war's end. (That was the one entitled simply, "The World War"—it not yet having been assigned a number, people feeling so certain there never could conceivably be another.) Discharged, returning home with a chest full of ribbons, his first employer made a job for the captain turned civilian in the Procurement Department. His hero days were over.

As a pencil pusher, he realized his duties were simply clerical; he wrote the orders but the requisitions came from Engineering. Even that early, Stann was made aware of why the experienced sales people tried to contact the engineers before the buyers who actually gave out the orders.

A noticeable knack for juggling words got him into advertising. There, among other well regarded ideas, thoughtful prescience had him suggesting listing metric equivalents along with the usual catalog measurements of the electro-mechanical devices which war conditions had made the manufacturer's major product line. Mr. D___, the general manager, told him to go ahead with it. He took books on mathematics from the library to help him develop the dualmetric and conventional English terms. Seminars were held for the company's salesmen to teach them how easy it was to move a decimal point instead of having to go through laborious calculations with fractions because in the metric system everything was based on multiples of tens.

It was a smart move. His foresight would help put his company far ahead of competition. Not until the late 1970's would American manufacturers start fully converting to the metric system, which enabled Stann's company to get a big jump on competition in foreign markets because of his foresight. His crystal ball, however, did not reveal what great impact this apparently unrelated idea would have on his life, to appear like heaven-sent many years later.

When a vacancy developed in the Sales Force, his standing request was filled; happily, he switched to outside sales. His six-foot frame was well fitted out in a new flannel gray suit. Topped by neatly trimmed wavy black hair, he now had much occasion to flash his dental ad gleaming tooth grin. He bought book after book having to do with various aspects of salesmanship, and took correspondence courses in business management. He fell in love. It was reciprocated. With his future seemingly assured, he married Helen G——, the attractive, very competent secretary to Mr. D——, the company's general manager, who good-heartedly gave them time off for a Niagara Falls honeymoon. In the next few years, two sons were born. Stann settled down presumably to the well defined routine of a family man and promising employee who had a bright future with a growing company. Well, man proposes, but . . .

One of the boys developed a serious arthritic condition. He would have to have relief from the rigors of the New England winters. Unhappily, but for the love of his child, Stann resigned his job and the family moved West, to settle in a small California town where they had intended to stop only long enough to visit Mort L., a favorite cousin of Helen's and the town's only banker.

Northlaking was a resort area popular for its great fishing. Watching the considerable number of sport fishermen passing through, Stann saw an opportunity for starting his own business. It wasn't the outside selling that he preferred but it looked too good to pass up. Politely refusing Mort's offer of a job in the bank, he opened a modestly stocked sporting goods store, Mort obligingly helped out with the financing. He got an appointment to issue fishing licenses, sold bait and stocked tackle calculated to catch the big ones.

The town prospered and grew. His business expanded. When the store next to his became vacant, he rented it to install a radio department by way of taking advantage of the country's latest enamorment. It was said the day would come when pictures could be sent through the air, just like radio, to be called "television." He listened thoughtfully, not entirely agreeing with the wiseacres who proclaimed it would never equal radio because one would have to remain seated in one spot to watch the program instead of allowing a person to move around the house and still hear the broadcasting; so, for lack of audiences, who would pay for the shows? He was able to discharge his indebtedness to Mort, even quit handling bait as not only messy but unseemly for his embryo department store. The world looked good to him.

As the years passed and the town's fame spread, came the manufacturers' sales representatives. Being a breed of men always on the lookout for new business, they sought out and found fruitful possibilities in the town and surrounding area. One of them, in the course of several trips through Northlaking, name of Harry L——, had become quite friendly with Stann. On one trip, he called to promote the virtues of a gold-plated antenna wire, an oddity but which nevertheless was to have a lively vogue because of its corrosion-resisting properties, considered especially desirable for coastal areas subject to salt air conditions.

A robust, cheerful man, with an engaging chuckle, Harry always had a story to relate. This time, discussing the antenna wire reminded him of an L.A. radio dealer named Leo Rolling, who was confronted with a prospect whom he had difficulty selling because the man insisted he wouldn't buy a radio until they made them so the music could go fast or slow like his Victrola. Eventually the fellow did buy the set but a few months later he ws back, complaining the radio was bringing in too much static.

"Where's your antenna — on the roof, I'll bet," asked Leo.

"Well, yes — stretched it from one corner to another."

"That's it, man! The cats have got at it."

"Cats?"

"Sure. You know how cats like to fool around on roofs. Just like they play with woolen string, they see these wires and they paw it it? They scratch it all up. Then, when your music comes along to travel down that wire, it comes to the torn spots and falls off. Between that and the cats banging at it — that's what makes your noise. What you need is a new roll of antenna wire — that'll fix it."

Stann roared. "And he bought it?"

"So help me! He did. This Leo — he's the character who paints white wash signs on his show windows reading, "In stock — VERY LOUD SPEAKERS."

As the rep flipped through his binder of catalogs, Stann noticed a thick section describing insulators, wire, machine screws and similar hardware.

"Does it really pay you to try and sell that nickel-and-dime stuff to stores like mine?" asked Stann curiously.

"No, of course not," frankly. "I sell through the wholesalers. But, I'm not one of those reps who stops at buying my distributor a lunch. When my products are on his shelves, it is my policy to help him move the goods. For one thing, I know the products better than his salesmen do, so, whenever possible I drop in on the dealers to educate their help to promote my lines, ultimately referring them to the distributors if they look like potential accounts. Some call it "missionary work" — in the drug sundries industry and such, it's "detailing the trade." And believe me — I make sure the distributor follows up on the referrals I give him!"

"But would it pay for them to send a salesman out here for the small amount of business I could give him?"

"Not for you alone. But he has other lines to sell and other prospects. There's the hardware store on Main Street, and that building supplies outfit the other side of town, the commercial fish cannery at the harbor, only twenty miles from here — there are lots of possibilities worth looking into. I think there's enough here to justify a distributor sending a man into this area — but it takes a rep like me to prove it to him. There are still some horse-and-buggy so-called distributors, you know, who consider themselves only warehouses, who sit on their duffs and wait for the business to walk in. They have to be prodded — not all, of course, but — "

"Is what you do regular practice with reps?"

Harry shrugged. "All I know is that in my product category, this happens to be one more way of irrigating a territory to help it grow. Maybe most reps wouldn't bother — a town like this — off their beaten tracks — " He grinned, pointing to the fishing rod on the back seat of his car. "In this case, it so happens, I can combine a little business with pleasure."

" 'Detailing the trade.' Interesting," mused Stann. It had not occurred to him that a manufacturers' agent might go that far in promoting the interests of his principals. Maybe such deep delving attention into the boondocks explained why this rep could afford to drive a Packard. It would seem one who does well by his principals and customers lives well. The incident was one he would have occasion to remember.

But in the period to follow, it was the immediate present that brought with it the beginning of calamity. The town's spectacular growth drew attention from afar. One of the country's famous chain of department stores built and moved into its own building, only two blocks from Stann's emporium, to feature prices in some cases even lower than his own costs. He was doomed.

Not at all concerned with Stann's business problems, Nature had its way with the couple. Helen gave birth to a baby girl. Something proved wrong with the child's legs, calling for a major operation or she would never be able to walk. The operation was successful but, along with the need for a lengthy period of after care, Stann was plunged deeply into debt. (How he would plump for family insurance in later years!) He folded up what was left of his business. Though at first sullenly refusing, he finally choked his pride down and accepted a job offered by the department store that had put him out of business. For the next five years, he was to function as a department manager and buyer.

He was a conscientious worker, paid well enough to enable him to make substantial reductions of his debts, to buy a house. It wasn't all good. He chafed under the unpleasant bickering that so often prevailed about him. In time, he was promoted to overseeing most of the store's buying but it was difficult to accept the imperious attitude of the pompous, pot-bellied store manager. For his temperament, the job was claustrophobic. He was restrained by the need for that sure monthly check, while he dreamed of the day when somehow he could change his occupation to outside selling.

In the meantime he was made the store's purchasing manager. In that capacity, he was called on by a steady stream of sales people, many of them independent professional salesmen. Prompted by now continually recurring thoughts, he asked callers searching questions about repping. Though scoffing to himself at the possibility of it ever being put to pragmatic use, nevertheless he set up a personal looseleaf notebook, whimsically inscribed with the title, "Some Day." At home evenings, he would make entries having to do with the operation of a sales agency.

Paying off final obligations incurred during his daughter's illness and trying to make the final payments on the mortgage on their home, made it necessary to husband every dollar. It was difficult to maintain subscriptions to the marketing publications that interested him, but a chance reference in one of his old business management books introduced him to the veritable library of excellent, wide-ranging literature available for free or at nominal cost from the government's Department of Commerce. He called upon the ever cooperative Helen and her secretarial experience to help organize a file and index system, it having become necessary to enlarge his notebook to a binder with three-inch capacity in which he listed subjects to which he felt he might "some day" want to refer. Helen was of an almost extinct species, the old fashioned wife, the kind who made her husband's career hers to join and to help make it go.

Heading for home one evening, he was slowed to a crawl by heavy traffic through the center of town. Concernedly he watched his gas gauge dropping toward "E," but it gave him an idea. It occurred to him that the town's urbanizing was providing an unusual opportunity for establishing a gas station in the downtown area. He thought of the last downtown vacant spots, two corner lots with "for sale" signs on them. Here was a chance to get into business for himself again — not what he really wanted, but probably the most sensible thing for a family man who was in no position to plunge into a risky career, who felt he could not exist with little or no income for a long period.

Real estate values had been escalating. It was easy to make a substantial loan on his now "clear" home and, again with Mort to lend him the balance needed, he drew up a deal for an independent gas station at the busy intersection. It was put together fast. Almost ready to open up, he was taking time out to dig into his brown bag lunch, while he watched the painter finishing the sign, "Clean rest stops here," which was to hang from the eaves of his station. Featuring such inviting slogans was still an innovation in those days. It would be a long time before gas stations generally, as a matter of course, would be providing luxurious, glistening, tile-walled facilities — unlocked, yet! — for enticing the traveling public to stop and use, in order to get their gas business.

Sometimes one indulges in a moment of relaxation from the urgencies of life, to drop the ballast of common sense while permitting one's mind to drift, envisioning ephemeral dreams floating colorfully through the air. Idly munching his sandwich, Stann visualized owning a chain of gas stations across the country. Perhaps he would get into politics eventually. No — too fantastic. He guessed what made more sense and more likely would be to accumulate enough money to see him through the beginning of a career in manufacturers' sales representation. Now, wouldn't that be something! He'd love that!

The painter departed, and the "clean restroom sign" now shining so invitingly had him chuckling as he was reminded of the story told him by the driver who had delivered his initial supply of gas the day before.

> The anecdote had to do with a big gas station and repair shop in L.A. where the driver had once worked as a mechanic. The firm was located on a diamond-shaped, downtown corner, the back portion given over to the operation of an extensive repair department, with the service area at the rear roofed over, an area far removed from the gas pumps at the corner. It was an open layout that simply invited hurrying pedestrians to short-cut across the vacant area from one street to the other. Warning signs were disregarded, people ducked between cars entering or leaving the premises. Not only were they creating hazards but a goodly number habitually cutting through the firm's lot had learned that the facilities provided for male employees were easily accessible.
>
> These "customers," paying no attention to the "employees only" sign, would squeeze through the small space close to the grease rack, with the oil tanks and the equipment presumably giving cover, to use the open, tin-walled urinal. Envisioning the possibility of a costly damage suit in case someone slipped and fell on the greasy floor, in any case hoping to do away

with the annoyance of these interlopers getting in the way of the employees at their work, the owner sardonically resorted to a quirk in human nature — peculiar, in this case, to the male Homo sapiens.

One of his children had brought home a most realistic metal reproduction of a common house fly, a novelty commonly sold in those days for joke purposes in variety stores featuring puzzles, games and such. He persuaded the youngster to let him have it, in exchange for a dollar.

The following day, he picked up a Ford Model T ignition coil from the parts replacement department. With one of his men's soldering irons, he affixed the metal fly to the urinal tin wall, about three feet above the gutter. An inconspicuous wire was soldered to the fly back of the wall, leading to the concealed spark coil. With some 20,000 volts output but of course at minute amperage, the arrangement was capable of supplying a small but unmistakable electric current.

His reasoning was simple. It is one of the facts of life that standing at that relieving wall, no man worthy of his manhood could conceivably resist aiming his stream at that fly. His feet plunked in the always damp, wet cement, the moment he hit the target a perfect circuit was completed. The resultant howling, backward leap had the crew breaking up in hysterical laughter. Embarrassed "customers" didn't care to return!

Eventually the hilarious setting had to be dismantled. It caused so much uproar and work stoppages while the men waited to watch the startled victim that the owner finally had to remove the fly. Eventually, the problem was solved by building an enclosure around the facility, with the entry from way in the back.

Problems of being a businessman!

Business went great from the start — for some six months. Sniffing the sweet smell of success, Stann could only hope one of several other non-competing possible kinds of business would take over the opposing corner. It was not to be. Along came one of the country's major oil companies, to install a spectacularly lighted, elaborately outfitted gas and service station across from Stann's place. Cutting his prices didn't accomplish much. In short order, he was reduced to ruefully watching streams of customers lined up in his rival's driveway whie his own business dwindled to more people coming in to use his restrooms than to buy gas.

He had no choice other than, after some negotiating, to accept an offer from another major oil company who wanted his location for one of their own stations. The deal enabled him to pay off most of his obligations, but not all. The wolf was at the door. The Manager of the department store whose job he had given up in disdain, coldly informed him that his old job was "satisfactorily filled." Stann turned to reading the help wanted ads; none seemed to work out. Debts began to pile up. The wolf had left puppies!

Ironically enough, a saving grace developed in the fact that the carpet baggers had moved in on his beloved town. To tide over until he could find something permanent, he took a job with a real estate developer. Having always enjoyed the challenges of selling, he was in his element, soon to be known as the group's star salesman, often patted on the back — literally — by his employer, one Horley J., a man in his sixties, hail-fellow-well-met, loud in affable mannerisms.

A somewhat awkward situation developed, however, in that Melsri, the office manager — and Horley's wife — also patted him but it was when no one else was in sight and it wasn't on the back. A good-looking man, now with a touch of gray to give him that well-known air of distinction, Stann was bound to draw any woman's admiring glances. In this case, unquestionably the boss' wife was a curvaceous, inviting woman (inviting in more ways than one!), much younger than her husband and quite openly flirtaceous.

Stann was no different from any normal man who could

still see when it came to viewing attractive female curves but, in this case, he would have preferred to admire the scenery at a distance. Like any married couple, Stann and Helen had experienced their unpleasant moments, there had been quarrels, but even at the height of exasperation, differences, they knew they loved each other. Theirs was an old-fashioned marriage. Stann had no interest in extra-curricular activities but there were times when bringing a customer into the office to close a deal made proximity with the office manager inevitable. To avoid embarrassing contacts was placing him in a strained position.

The situation resolved itself unexpectedly. None of the staff knew it other than Horley and Melsri but the developer was following a practice that cost financial institutions thousands before they caught up with him. One of the most flagrant rip-offs was to construct a property for which a loan of, say, $10,000 had been wangled from a bank. The building finished, the developer's total cost might be no more than $8,000, so all he had to do was find someone to buy the property—regardless of ability to pay or how little down payment—just so the buyer would assume the $10,000 loan, and the builder would be off the hook with a $2,000 profit. There were other more subtle variations on such crude flim-flams, ultimately to be wiped out by protective laws.

In the meantime, however, the shenanigans landed Horley in prison, his wife eloped with one of the other salesmen, and Stann was once more out "looking."

With three years gone by as superintendent of the nearby fish cannery, Stann felt he had reason to consider this job fairly permanent. He visualized the final clearance of all his obligations, to get ahead a bit, perhaps to get into real estate himself some day. Why not? He lived in a continually growing community and with a little capital he could foresee a good future . . . that would have the advantage of getting him on the outside, selling . . .

Once again, Fate intervened. He arrived at the plant one day, to find pickets stationed at the entrance. The cannery owner, one Rick M., a man of huge proportions, surly, penny-pinching, spat on the floor when Stann tried to reason with him in behalf of the men's grievances. The issue was a simple one. The plant did not have sufficient extra cold storage facilities for keeping an exceptionally large catch until it could be processed within normal hours. Perhaps once or twice in several months then, it would become necessary for the crews to work nights and weekends. Rick had steadily refused to pay overtime rates upon those occasions.

"Don't try to tell me, college boy!" Rick roared out a vehement, "When work is slack, and they got nuthin' to do but shoot craps and drink beer, do they refund me any of the money I pay 'em—for doin' nuthin'? The bastards—they got good jobs workin' for me—they don't like it, they go someplace else."

Stann continued to remonstrate. "And suppose a big catch comes in while the men are on strike—what would you do? You think you can hire replacements? From where? They'll break you!"

It was useless. Stann sighed. When an irresistible force meets an immovable, stubborn old bastard of a body . . . It was one more lesson from life for him, this time in the principles and operations of unionism when one side or the other is patently unreasonable. . . . The strike was prolonged, turned bitter. The jut-jawed employer refusing to budge, the men just as stubbornly staying out, finally resulted in the cannery being put out of business and the superintendent out of a job.

Stann wasn't embittered so much as bewildered by the roller coaster ups and downs of life beyond his control. He had an engineering education but he hadn't gone that route because, for one thing, he wasn't the type who would be happy hunched over a drawing board for the rest of his life. He wasn't ingenious in a technical sense. He loved people, he enjoyed getting out among them, he always felt selling was a great way to make a living — but, somehow, Fate seemed to have singled him out to make it so difficult for him to maintain his family in decent life-style, to educate his children, to keep up with his normal obligations. It was hard to accept the spirit-grinding domination and effect on his life of ignorant straw bosses such as this last example.

Each of us is concerned primarily with one's little ole self. Stann just still hadn't realized how commonplace, how widespread were such trials among millions in the business world. It was particularly in such unhappy moods that the longing for "Some Day" would surface, when he wished fervently he could be in business for himself. He would clench his fists and dream of being a rabbit able to spit in the lion's eye if the spirit so moved him.

But all was changed when an interruption to his dreams came along in the form of a proposition he could not refuse.

Helen had kept in touch with an old friend and fellow employee back in their home town, whose husband was still working for the manufacturer who had first employed Stann. A letter had arrived in which she spoke of how greatly the company had grown. With the impetus war had given, this manufacturer of electro-mechanical devices had become a prosperous company now employing many hundreds. Her husband mentioned overhearing Mr. D., the general manager, speaking of how fortuitous it was that they had once had an employee who had made the metric system standard usage for the company, long before competition got around to it, and how he wished he could hire more men with such foresight. She had recalled who he was talking about! With this favorable remembrance of Stann's ability, would it be an idea for him to contact Mr. D. about returning to perhaps a very good position?

It was to be a timely suggestion. The boys were living in Los Angeles. His health long restored, Junior had taken his MBA and was working as a well paid bookkeeper while preparing for his CPA exams. Billy, the number two son, had gone in for a career in insurance. Like his father, he enjoyed selling and already ranked among the high volume producers of business for his company.

Only Dorothy, who had turned out to be an exceptionally beautiful girl, was still living with her parents. Even she was making enough money for her needs at odd jobs—baby sitting, typing manuscripts and reports for a secretarial group. So, why not? It was the period in the early '50s, when skilled help was scarce. A brief correspondence with Mr. D., who remembered him very well, resulted in an attractive offer. He wired his acceptance.

It was easy to sell the house. He soon found himself back working for the people with whom he had started in the business world, again temporarily as a buyer, with the same promise—presumably, as soon as possible, he would be put on the staff as an outside salesman.

This time, it didn't work out that way.

Whenever an opening in Sales did develop, Purchasing was always short-handed just at that moment and he could not be spared. The years passed. He was moved up to Director of Purchasing. His friend Mr. D. retired. A distant figure, Mr. P., the founder and president of the company, was forced to return, to take over running it again, much to that gentleman's annoyance. For some years now, he had left things pretty much to his general manager, which had permitted him to enjoy his affluence, traveling from one to another of the lush pleasure spots of the world.

Impelled by force of habit rather than with any more real expectations, Stann's "Some Day" hobby had steadily grown thicker with observations and lessons culled from conversations with the independent sales agents who called.

But for him, it was all on the back burner. He had what most people would have considered a highly desirable position. He hadn't forgotten the misery of being out of work, of suffering financial straits. The general manager's position was going unfilled; he had as good a chance for it as anybody, he reasoned, soon as Mr. P. had his fill of working again.

How many men recognize what Stann faced: how does one give up not only the presumed certainties of a well paying position but with imminent possibilities of being promoted to the very highest echelon of management? Perhaps it was true, as statistics had it, that four out of five men were in the wrong jobs, but to exchange what he had for the scary plunge into the deep, uncharted shoals of self-employment? Yet, somehow, the attraction of being his own boss, of a career in independent sales representation, never lost its appeal. Almost unconsciously, his secret ambition influenced much of his day-to-day life.

As a buyer, Stann was far from the commonplace run-of-the mill paper jockey. Aside from being a gregarious person by nature, always happily making new friends, he was a prominent member of the local purchasing agents' association. Instinctively he realized the pragmatic value for a man in business taking part in his industry's trade associations. He would volunteer to work on committees and willingly accepted officerships which many evaded because the chores were time consuming, and carried with them a measure of responsibility to fellow contemporaries. In addition to buyers of electro-mechanical products, he never overlooked an opportunity to lunch with any of the area's buyers from industries other than his own, to cultivating their friendship. He acquired wide acquaintance with the territory's activities, tried to memorize as many names as possible of key personnel, studying sales volume figures of the various companies, the categories of products they were likely to buy and, in general, steeping himself to whatever extent possible in familiarity with their buying policies. His "Some Day" was becoming encyclopedic.

Sometimes, when shaving, he scoffed at his image. "Just a schizophrenic! My job? Buying! My ambition? Selling! How does a man walk two sides of the same street?" Despite its impracticality, he continued to dream of some vague, undefined future. But when you are in your late forties, pushing the fifties, that future has a way of breaking the sound barrier in its rush to become the present.

One can be certain of only one thing in life—nothing is certain. With the lack of warning and devastating shock of an earthquake, Stann's world suddenly broke up, to leave him gasping on the brink of disaster. Overnight, the sure job vanished. Stunned, once again he was among the unemployed. It was in the 1950s, when an uncommon word, CONGLOMERATE, began to loom up familiarly on the American financial scene. In secret negotiation, the privately owned company for which Stann had worked so long was absorbed by a group taking over a number of the country's long established corporations. President P. received a huge sum for his ownership and disappeared from his former employee's lives. New management moved in. Stann received two weeks extra pay and a polite note telling him his services would no longer be required. Dazed, scarcely able to grasp the fact that he once again had been crushed by circumstances beyond his control, Stann set out doggedly looking for a job.

What followed became an all-too-familiar story in many a household. To secure a position commensurate with his experience, his capabilities, comparable to the status of the work he had been doing, proved completely out of the question for a man who had reached what was once known as middle age. He tried. Unabashedly, he let friends know he was in search of a position; he followed up every lead, all to no avail. The months went by. They sold the second car as expenses continued, his bank account dwindled, resources were being steadily depleted. The situation was approaching desperation. Still unwilling to believe his luck wouldn't turn, he took out a loan on his home to live on, the property on which he had made the last payment so happily just the year before.

Helen was a tremendous reader. She had acquired an enormous vocabulary which manifested itself in shy attempts to compose poetry. She had been an enthusiastic participant in the local art club, largely because, as another hobby, she had taken up the sculptor's mallet and had been having fun creating more or less recognizable metallic figures. But all that had to be forgotten now. Despite Stann's protests, she determinedly set about seeking a job. She ran into the same discouraging obstacle—her age was against her.

One day came a break. Through a friend from the art club, she was introduced to the owner of a popular restaurant who, it developed, had an opening for a cashier. To her joy, it turned out that this man *preferred* a woman of advanced age, believing she would prove more responsible in handling his cash register than the youthful types. A short wait while he checked references, and she got the job.

Stann shook his head morosely. "It's been eight months now." They had kept their plight from the children. The boys were doing all right. Dorothy was making her beauty count, having started to do well on her own as a high fashion model in New York. "Guess I'm the only crack in the glass in this family," he muttered.

Helen took the reproduction of the sculptor's mallet from the mantel which she had won as a prize in one of her art club's exhibitions. She brandished it in her husband's face. "Aren't you the philosopher who said: "the hammering a man gets in the business world is only to prove he can take it?"

She punched the mallet into the palm of her left hand. "Another way to say it," she mused, "is that under life's forces, a man reacts like material under the sculptor's mallet. If base, it will crack and break, and so will he, but if made of true stuff, the hammering will only serve to pound him into shape . . . Hey—how about that?"

Stann managed to smile. "You really put that well—and you're right, I guess—except that right now, that hammering has got me punchy. I just can't think any more."

"I'll say you can't! Why, for cryin' out loud, here you are facing the opportunity of your life—what you've always dreamed of doing—"

"What in the hell are you talking about?"

"Just what *you* have always been talking about! About how you always wanted to be a manufacturers' sales representative! So here's your chance! The salary I'm getting won't enable us to live high, but it's enough to keep beans on the table until you get going, until you've acquired enough paying lines—"

Stann's jaw dropped. As the full import of her words finally penetrated, he leaped to his feet and enveloped her in his arms. "Listen, you! I've seen you with your clothes off! Where have you been keeping your wings? Or did you just now today turn into an angel?" He waltzed her around the room. "My God, what have I done to deserve a woman like this?"

He released her, to start excitedly pacing the floor. "You are so right! I have been taking a stiff course in the School of Life, but I've learned! I've dealt with most every kind of business, with all kinds of people—had all kinds of experiences with them. I've been *preparing* to become a professional salesman. And now, with a little more study of the techniques—there must be books I haven't seen yet—you've made it possible for me to start!"

They spent the rest of the evening poring through his "Some Day." When he came to the section referring to acquaintances in the purchasing association, he made a classified list of the names and figures he had noted, along with tabulations of the manufacturers with whom he had dealt as a purchasing agent, scrupulously omitting those who had independent reps calling on him. In the latter instance, he didn't need any written code of ethics to realize their principals were not to be contacted if he expected to take a legitimate place in the world of independent professionals. A code called the "golden rule" he felt covered that situation.

His name as the company's former Purchasing Agent, was frostily recognized by the new sales manager's secretary but, he assured her, he was not back seeking a job, only that he had a matter of special interest for her boss and that was why he wanted the interview. After a short wait, he was admitted to the executive's office.

At home that evening, he roared with laughter as he had not for many months. "It was like shooting fish in a barrel," he told the delighted Helen. "Hard at it—revamping the company's selling methods—this sales manager was just considering the possibilities of changing from direct salesmen to the independent rep system.

"I spoke of my many years of experience in so many phases of business. I reeled off the names of numerous guys I knew as friends among the local buyers, along with figures of their purchases, of yearly sales volume, of buying practices and all that. I displayed my familiarity with the territory and conditions—and, of course, I know the line forward and backwards. Was he impressed—wow! He all but begged me to take the line on for this territory—on a 10% commission basis. It won't be a big line, hon—but it's a start. There'll be others—I'm on my way—finally!"

REINCARNATION — or,
FATHER OF A BRAINCHILD

"It became a new life for me, Harry," said Stann, "a second time around. I felt I was reincarnated, born into a new existence, to gratify creative instincts, to dream up blueprints for achievement and to carry them out." He sipped his coffee. "Sound silly?"

"Hell, no! You're talking to an old-time rep himself, you know."

Absently, Stann smeared mustard on his hot dog. "I wonder if it's the wish that fathers the brainchild. How does one explain the creation of circumstances that enables one to bring a dream into reality, to have something new that never existed before? Maybe you conceive a child. Or invent an ingenious mechanical device. Or design a bridge using an engineering principle unknown before."

"If you could answer such questions, you'd have the explanation for the mystique of success," commented Harry.

Stann's introspection continued. "In my first existence, I created a family. In my second, I constructed an institution," he grinned, " — if I may be forgiven for the implication of gigantic size — although, it *is* a company employing something like twenty people — which will be going on long after I am gone."

"Twenty people?" echoed Harry admiringly. This he understood! "Wow — you did make a success of it, didn't you!"

They were leaning on the counter of one of the temporary eating places installed at selected spots in the exhibition hall. A cacophony of voices, characteristic of trade conventions, roared in the background as they stood at the quickie lunch counter, eathing their sandwiches. Visiting crowds filled the aisles, to stop and gaze at the colorful exhibitions, to engage the booth attendants in conversation, to ogle shapely girls hired for the occasion as they passed out the souvenir knickknacks and the catalogs always prominent at trade conventions.

Stann had accidentally bumped into his friend. They stared as each tried to recall where he had known the other. Harry got it first. "Last time I saw you was in that little California fishing town — I was promoting radio accessories while on a fishing trip — "

"Right! Gosh, what a memory. That goes back — "

"And come to think of it, I've often read items about you in the trade papers — you evidently made a big success of repping — and in a remarkably short time. It took me thirty years at it before I could retire. So — have you made your first million?"

"Well — actually — a little better than that," grinned Stann. "I've had some terrific lines. Got enough so that I decided to quit. Reason Helen and I are in New York is we're about to board the 'Royal Oceana' tomorrow, starting on a three months cruise around the world. She wanted to do some shopping so I thought I'd drop in here for a couple of hours, maybe run into some old friends, just as happened with you. My son Billy, who came to work with us abut five years ago, is taking over the business."

"Great! But tell me — how in the world did you get going so quick — especially considering how people think men over thirty ought to be embalmed!"

Stann spoke of his dreams, of his preparatory notebook "Some Day" and his voluminous files on the various aspects of independent marketing. "Nothing brilliant," he said. "Just preparing for what didn't seem too likely." He told of the abrupt change in his life, of how he acquired his first line, with Helen supporting them while he struggled to build a business. "It came to me that with all the experience a man gains in business life, that 'how-to' which comes only with the years, just had to have value if presented in the right way. I bragged abut my age rather than trying to hide it — in that fact alone, without even saying so, the implication was lots of know-how. I singled out manufacturers who were employing their own salesmen, to point up the advantages of a professional salesman system. There were those who saw it. My best lines—the real biggies—came from such sources."

"You always were sales minded." Harry took a bite out of his cheese sandwich and grimaced. "Tastes like wallboard! These convention sandwiches! But, anyhow—with so many sales managers so much younger than you, how did you persuade—"

"I had better luck with the younger than with the older guys. I emphasized my understanding of the customers' problems, who would be my targets, because *I had been there*—as an experienced buyer myself, as a small businessman, as an employee, as one who knows how to deal with people. Many of these young fellows have the degrees but they are still conscious of authority vested in older men, associating the wisdom of the older man with their professors, with the father whom they had looked up to for so long. Age still carries with it the aura of wisdom."

He grinned at Harry's raised skeptical eyebrows. "Of course—I admit—it didn't fly with all of them. Many a six-foot erstwhile football hero, not long off the field, feels his stature is increased to ten feet tall when he becomes an executive in the business world. But—I was successful in finding enough intelligent sales managers to build up a small but beautiful roster of lines. And—on each of them—I made my promises good."

Harry shook his head. "Wonderful!"

"Well, old timer—it's been great seeing you—but I guess Helen will be waiting for me at the hotel—I'd better run."

"Certainly glad I ran into you, Stann—and congratulations on the success of your career—couldn't happen to a nicer guy. Have a wonderful trip!"

"Thanks, pal. We'll have to get together after I get back. So long." □

Well, friends —

This winds up my library on the subject of independent manufacturers' sales representation. I've enjoyed the writing but, over that, I've been made most happy by so many gratifying comments from readers.

I've been told of continual reference to them, of reading and re-reading various chapters, of finding the books helpful in one way or another, of favorable impact on careers — great for my ego but, over all, I can only repeat what I said in introducing the first volume:

"The rep business has been good to me. I hope it does as much for you, if not more. And if my book helps, in any degree — well, that's why it was written."

Good luck!

Sincerely,
Frank De Vell